After You Were Gone

Urfana Ayub

adam ayub

Adam Ayub Publications

Published by:
Adam Ayub Publications
Copyright© Urfana Ayub 2016

Translator - Dr Zahid Hussain
Editor - Siobhan Dignan
Cover Art - integritiphotography.com

Published by Adam Ayub Publications, Unit 2B Listers Mill, Heaton Road, Heaton, Bradford, West Yorkshire, BD9 4SH

www.adamayubpublications.co.uk
www.adamayub.co.uk

Printed By Mega Printing in Turkey

'After You Were Gone' was first published in April 2011 in the Urdu language, attracting many messages of praise from readers worldwide.

"After You Were Gone is a very impressive book. On one hand it speaks of the sudden and untimely death of an adolescent son and on the other hand it portrays a beautiful picture of being submissive to God's will. Mrs Urfana Ayub is a very courageous lady. She has written this book amidst grief and tears. It explicitly illustrates a mother's infinite love for her son and eloquently speaks of her conviction and strength.

Through this book she has conveyed a message of mankind's humility and the everlasting power of God, which will, God willing, have its impact on its readers. Reading this book with insight also reveals the basic truth that man should never err to be forgetful of God's remembrance and he should indulge in perseverance under all circumstances."

Dr. Musharraf

"God knows best. I know we never lose the people we love. They live the rest of our lives with us in our hearts. My words are not adequate to express the sorrow I feel for you. Adam was an inspiration to everyone around him. After reading the book I feel as though I'm the blessed one to have been graced by your son's big heart and his inviting personality (it is truly a mark of wonderful parents). May your memories give you strength."

Alisha

"You are an inspiration to us. I do feel your pain just as I feel my sister's pain when she lost her son. God Willing you will have a house in heaven for your patience. You will always have your son's memories."

Robina

"Assalam-o-Alaikum! Yesterday I happened to come across your both books in Army Central Library Rawalpindi. Being an Army Officer I often visit this place in search of valuable books for my soul's satisfaction. I must pay rich tributes to you on taking such a courageous step by writing on such a topic which gave you immense grief and loss.

Believe me, by reading your books I travelled along with Mr Adam.

May God Almighty give him a place in heaven. Your children are lucky that they have a mother like you. Once again my heartiest compliments to you on writing such emotional masterpiece based on a true event of your life. I pray for you and your family to God to grant patience and uncounted blessings."

Farrukh

"After reading your book "Taray Janay Kay Baad" I know you as much as I know myself. I felt you are not writing for yourself but are expressing my feelings, my words, my thoughts and what I am going through. It's all because of my son Zain. You would not believe the resemblance of Adam and Zain and the similarity of your feeling and mine; what I am going through because I too lost the one who made me mother for the first time. My son aged just 23 died on 7th May 2015 after Morning Prayer in my arms."

Lubna

"I wanted to say how I have admired your strength and resilience in the face of this huge loss. It is humbling to see you turn your inner grief into outward positivity. Not a lot of people have that courage or determination. Your book is an intriguing, interesting and emotive insight into a mother's life and our being. The description of the family's grief, reactions, coping strategies and how they managed without Adam, someone who had a special position within the family, was heartfelt. You have portrayed his character, personality, mannerisms and fun-loving sense of humour and your love for him well. I had to open this book a few times and then close it because of the impact it had on me. Although I was reading about your loss and grief as Adam's mother and family, it also affected me too. This could be me, or anyone who has endured loss of loved one that has had such a major impact. A reminder, that this world is a temporary abode."

Amina

"Amazing, heart - touching story. I loved it. While I was reading the book, I was dying to sleep and yawning but wanted to reach the last page...You are an amazing and superb writer."

Sarah

"I read the book in the last two consecutive nights and each time I found it hard to put it down and kept on reading it until either I was too upset or too tired to continue with it. I found your narratives very moving and touching. I am sure it would be great help and great resource of therapy to many in a similar situation."

Yasmin

"Simple phrases, but with strong emotions and religious quotations that are brilliant and can support any grieving person in their deepest time of need."

Dr Sadia

"Heartbreaking to read, as anyone who has lost someone will know the feeling of overwhelming emotions and moments relived. At the same time it was a comfort to know that such a situation can bring positive change and even more love and unity in the family, All praise be to God."

Asad

"Not just a book with a strong message but written from the heart. Very emotional piece of writing. Brought tears to my eyes. A mother's story from the heart. The words used are very inspiring. I am sure this book will touch thousands of hearts. It certainly melted mine. Your son was a blessing to you and your family. So every moment you spent with him will be special not only to you, but to your entire family. I feel you are very lucky to be very close to one another as a family. Not many people are lucky to be this way."

Tasneem

"An interesting read. May God truly reward Urfana for sharing her pain (karb) with her readers. I have learnt profound life lessons. Had I not about her refelctive experience."

Bint e Bano

"After You Were Gone' (Taray Janay Kay Baad), is full of strong emotions it's a story of a mother who shared her feelings after losing her eldest son, who was her friend. It wasn't easy for me to read the book, the book is clearly a message of hope and courage and a reminder for many as the "reality and purpose of life".

Qasim

Adam Ayub
May 7, 1991 - December 27, 2009

DEDICATION

I dedicate these pages to my beloved friend and deceased son, Mohammed Adam Ayub, who is no more in this world by the command of our Lord. Though his life was short, his memory will remain the best asset of my life.

Urfana Ayub

By Mahnoor Hasnat and Asadullah

Preface

I belong to the beautiful city of Karachi in Pakistan. I am the only sister of four brothers. My father is a retired Pakistani Naval officer. My mother is a housewife and she is a very virtuous and religious woman.

My childhood memories are a valued treasure for me. I still cherish those beautiful memories. I am so grateful to Allah Almighty, who has always showered me with His grace and mercy. He blessed me with parents who were very loving and affectionate. Undoubtedly, they brought me up the best possible way. They went beyond their means to provide me and my brothers with both contemporary and religious education; they taught us etiquette and values. When I look back at my past, it seems as though I was a delicate china doll whose parents cherished her a lot and fulfilled her every wish. I do not remember a single wish or dream that was not fulfilled. My parents showed more confidence and pride in me than they did in their sons. With gratitude to Allah (SWT) I never breached their trust either.

Life before marriage seemed like a fairy tale to me. I got married to my cousin Mohammed Ayub at the age of nineteen and moved to Bradford, Yorkshire, England. A year after our marriage, God bestowed motherhood upon me and blessed me with a very beautiful son. My son suffered from heart problems since birth. He had his first heart operation at the age of one year, which was successful.

My son, Mohammed Adam Ayub, was the first grandson on both the maternal and paternal sides, and was loved dearly by both families. After Adam, Allah (SWT) blessed me with another son, Mohammed Arslan, then a daughter, Ambar, and then another son, Mohammed Ahmad. By the grace of God, all three of them are fine and healthy. Adam used to go to hospital regularly for his check-ups, and underwent major heart surgery at the age of five. God Almighty saved his life at that time.

My life was passing very peacefully like still waters. Then suddenly there was a storm in this still sea which stirred everything up in our previously serene lives. Adam was feeling unwell for the previous few days. As his stomach was hurting and he was also being sick, I took him to hospital for a check-up. Within a few hours of being in the hospital, my child passed away in my presence.

This book is about the journey I went through from 27th December 2009 to 27th December 2010. This book is an expression of the pain, distress and anguish I endured during that year and about the knowledge and experience which I gained from Adam's death. This book is also about the feelings that shook my faith up and about the pain a mother felt on losing her son. Above all, this book is an eternal source of reward from God for Adam. All the income from my story will go to charitable causes. You are also contributing to this noble cause by purchasing this book.

Every page has my feelings, pain, anguish, memories and fragrance of my son: what he said, his going away, his funeral, his grave. Most of all, this book is a means to thank the Almighty who gave me a chance to write something, to share my sorrow, grief and bereavement with others and to convey my message to people; the message He gave me by calling my Adam back. A mother has tried to write down her son's last moments and the beautiful memories of his life. This book is about my heart, my thoughts, my feelings and my actions. It is based on truth. Through this book, I wish to show my gratitude towards the people who are playing a very important role in one way or the another in my life. After all the blessings from the Almighty, who I am and where I am today are because of these people.

First of all, I would like to mention my mother, Zahida Nasreen. She is the one who has always been a role model for me. Whatever I am today is because of the upbringing by this great woman; no doubt this was by the grace of God. The second person is my father, Mohammed Ishaque. My father brought me up with great care and tenderness. I had the best childhood one could have. I was pampered like a princess. He is a very God-fearing and righteous person who has complete faith in his Lord. If one half of my personality is a reflection of my mother, the other half is that of my father. I am proud to be their daughter.

How marvellous these family relationships and feelings are! I remember when my mother sent me two diaries which she had written down herself in my memory, in which she had gathered together many of her own poems, verses, prayers and quotes for me. Back then I wondered how a mother could spare so much time for her children. Now I realise all that my mother did for me, when I myself began writing after losing my child. How was it that I could write? I was not familiar with writing poetry. Yet I was able to compose my first Urdu and English poem for my lost child.

This book has given me a chance to thank every family member, whether on my parents' side or my in-laws, who gave me strength, courage and support during those difficult times, so that I could take care of and gather myself. This was especially true of my three children, Arslan, Ambar and Ahmad. In addition, due to the presence of my husband Ayub's mother and father, I did not feel the absence of my own parents in those difficult times. May Allah (SWT) bless them with a healthy and happy life full of faith and may they see all the happy occasions in the lives of their children.

Where all these people provided support for me, there is the name of one person who I specially want to mention to whom

I am grateful from the bottom of my heart. This is Ayub's sister, Farhat, who I look upon also as my own daughter as well as a sister, who, in those very difficult times, took care of me, wiped my tears and held my hand.

Had I not found support, love and courage from all of these loved ones, I would have broken down or shattered because of the death of my eldest adult son. Their loving touch kept me in one piece.

The most important among all is my husband, Mohammed Ayub, without whose love and encouragement, it would perhaps not have been possible for me to take the step of writing this book.

If you want to contact me and give me your valuable feedback, you can reach me at this email address:

adamayubbooks@gmail.com

Contents

1. Snowfall and Sickness

Saturday, 26th December, 2009

My eldest son Adam had been feeling unwell for the last three to four days. He would throw up whatever he ate. He had a stomachache and his back was also hurting, so he asked me to massage it. I thought his stomach was hurting probably because he had not had anything to eat. I urged him repeatedly to have a medical check-up but he kept on saying, "No, I am fine".

My four children had been on Christmas holidays from school since 21st December and I had also taken two weeks leave from work to spend time with them. It snowed all that first week. I spent this time at home with my children. Due to the five days of snowfall, we did not go anywhere out of the house until the 25th. It was a Friday, Christmas Day, and the weather was milder. We went to Ammi's (my mother - in - law's) place. My husband Ayub also had a day off from work. We spent the entire day at Ammi's home. In the evening, we also attended the birthday party of my niece, Huma.

All day long, Adam was feeling very lethargic and also was complaining of a stomachache and feeling sick. Ayub took him to a doctor at the local health centre. The doctor prescribed tablets to stop him from vomiting. After taking the tablets, Adam stopped being sick, but he still would not eat anything. We returned home that evening. The next day, Saturday the 26th, Uncle Abid, Auntie Zeenat and their children came to pay a surprise visit to Adam. Later during the day, Uncle

Mohammed, Auntie Erum and their children also came to visit Adam. Adam still had no energy or appetite, but was feeling better than before, though he was still not his usual lively and busy self. As a first year university student studying for a youth and community degree, he led a full and very active life.

Mamoon (maternal uncle) had brought a box of chocolates for Adam, which he did not even open. Uncle Abid had brought fruit, which he perhaps took a little bite of. While Adam was watching a football match, I was asking him to go to hospital to have a check-up and to make sure everything was all right. Adam is 18, so his parents can no longer make medical decisions for him.

He agreed and said, "Let the match finish and then we will go".

Ayub, our daughter Ambar and I were observing the fast of 9th of Muharram, the first month of the Islamic Lunar Year. I was thinking, Ayub will take Adam to hospital once the fast ends at sunset.

For the last few years I had not been accompanying my son to the hospital. It was his father who took him for check-ups or appointments, or sometimes Abbu (my father-in-law) would go along. It was a strange co-incidence that on this occasion Adam insisted, "Mum, come with me please".

At first I declined saying that, "Dad is going with you, you will be back soon after the check-up". But when he insisted, I changed my mind and went with them to the hospital.

My three younger children Ambar (age 14), Arslan (15) and Ahmad (10) were busy baking in the kitchen. I called them out and said, "We will be back soon. Come and see your brother. We are going to the hospital".

They rushed to the door, said goodbye, and hurried back inside. They must have been thinking that he would be back soon. Had they known that he would never set his foot back into this house?

Whenever Adam went to the hospital he would first visit his grandmother. Her home was on the way to the hospital. This time when we went there he waved to Dadi Ammi (grandmother), Baba (grandfather), Phuphie (father's sister) and his aunties through the car window, and after saying goodbye to everyone, my son left for hospital.

When we reached Leeds General Infirmary, it was almost 6 p.m. By now Adam felt very tired. He asked Dad, "Can you please bring me a wheelchair? I will not be able to walk that far". Ayub brought a wheelchair and Adam was seated in it. We had to wait for a little while in the waiting area, but were quickly seen.

When the doctor asked Adam, "Where does it hurt?", he answered that, besides the stomachache, it had been hurting all over his body and he was also having a little bit of trouble with breathing. The hospital staff immediately put an oxygen mask on him and chest x-rays were done. The doctor told us that Adam had a chest infection which had spread widely and turned into pneumonia. Immediately antibiotics were given intravenously via a drip. After examining his lungs, the doctor also told us that a lot of fluid had collected in and around them.

Adam was immediately taken to Ward No.17 where they performed various blood tests and monitored his heart. But after a few hours they brought the heartbreaking news that he was not going to make it.

I could not believe what I heard when the doctor uttered the words, "He cannot get through this."

I asked the doctor what it was due to. Was it because of pneumonia or his heart condition?

He replied that firstly, the pneumonia had spread so widely that Adam's heart, already being weak, could not pump blood for the whole body, and secondly, he had so much fluid around his lungs. "We will take the fluid out and hope it might do some good."

The doctor numbed Adam's skin in front of me. I was holding my child against my body at that time and I was also holding both his hands. During all this time, Adam was drowsy and he had the oxygen mask on his face. It did not appear that the procedure to drain the lungs had hurt him; that part of his body had become totally numb. They drilled his lungs in front of me and with a thick needle took out about three big bowls of fluid. I just wondered whether it was possible to have so much fluid inside one's stomach and that was probably why his stomach was hurting and Adam had not been eating or drinking anything.

After an hour or two, the medical team did another scan of the lungs and found that more fluid had collected. By this time the doctors had lost hope completely. Nothing seemed to be functioning normally, including Adam's blood pressure and heart rate. They told us to have a "Family Time" and call whoever we wanted to.

I phoned and informed everyone. They started arriving; everybody came. Grandfather, Grandmother, aunts and uncles from both sides of the family, their wives. Adam's brothers and sister also arrived.

Adam kept on asking for water. At first the doctors had totally refused it, but then gave us permission to moisten a cotton wool ball and either wet his lips with it or drip water into his mouth drop by drop with this soaked cotton wool ball. This I kept on doing. Later, they allowed him to have little sips of water through a straw. I gave him holy water (*Zam Zam*).

I encouraged my child to recite the *Kalima*[1] with me. He was almost drowsy, but I kept on saying, "Adam, my son, say it in your heart". He was not speaking at all. Everybody encouraged him to recite the Declaration of Faith with them. He tried to say something once or twice, but his voice failed him. I felt utterly helpless.

Adam gestured for his mobile and texted on it "Lucozade Sports Drink". Ayub rushed downstairs to the canteen to get the drink. The shop was closed, but the doctor brought the drink for us and I gave it to Adam to sip it slowly.

He tried to text again but this time his fingers failed him. I kept on asking him, "Do you need anything my child?" or if he wanted to say something. While sitting beside him, involuntarily my tears were streaming. When I kissed him he opened his eyes and wiped my tears with his hands and gestured to me not to cry. When I got up, Dad sat there. He was also crying, and kissed Adam. Adam wiped his tears as well and gestured to him not to cry.

When Grandmother came and asked, "Do you know who has come to see you, Adam?", he nodded. Even at this late stage it appeared that he had his senses. He knew what was happening around him. Everybody caressed him and talked to him. His Phuphie (paternal aunt) talked to him, conveyed Uncle Babur's love to him and encouraged him recite the Kalima with her.

---

1   *Declaration of the Islamic faith*

16

As he drank the Zam Zam, Adam found his voice. He asked, "Where is my dad?", and when the nurse came, he asked, "What time will I get breakfast?"

It was 6 a.m. The nurse said the breakfast will be served at 7 a.m. "What would you like to have?"

Adam said, "Toast". He kept on putting his finger in his mouth; so hungry was my child. His hunger was unbearable for him. Suddenly it looked like his breathing had stopped. I called the doctor. He explained that though Adam is breathing, he has only minutes to live and will leave us at any moment.

After the doctor left, I kissed and hugged Adam with all my heart. My child asked me very clearly, "What did the doctor say?" and, "Why are you crying Mum?" I comforted him. These were the last few words he spoke.

Then it looked like he was reclining towards his left side. That is, his gaze, his neck and his body were leaning towards the left. I straightened him many times on his pillow but he would again turn his neck towards the left. Now Adam was starting to get restless and kept on pulling his oxygen mask off. As it was pre-dawn and also as he was under the influence of medicines, Adam had been sleepy for a long while, but now he was opening his eyes and continued looking towards his left. It appeared as though he was seeing something which I could not see.

All of a sudden, it looked as if my son had stopped breathing and his gaze had become fixed. I started weeping, my heart was restless, and I called the doctor. I was crying and saying, "Ayub, my child has gone! Ayub, my child has gone!"

Doctors and nurses rushed over. They asked us to go to the Parents' Room. They pressed on Adam's chest to restore his breathing and did whatever was possible for them to do. They said he was breathing, but I cannot express what I felt at that moment. I already knew it in my heart: "Urfana, your child has returned back to his Creator."

I called my children who had already visited their brother and gone home. I called them back again so that they could once again meet their brother. When I came back and looked at Adam and kissed him, his gaze was completely lifeless and his eyes had become dark red as if they were filled with blood. Both eyes were half open, but his body looked lifeless.

The doctors discussed among themselves and told us it was the drips and the life support machine which were keeping him the way he was. What they meant was he was breathing with the aid of machines and he could depart at any time. In a way, he was suffering and had no chance of survival.

"Now the choice is yours", the doctor informed us, "because he will go in any case, but if we reduce the dose, he would suffer less".

Ayub and I both decided that we did not want our child to suffer. The moment they reduced the dose, my child, the love of my life, breathed the last breath of his life in front of me. My child had actually left this world. I was shocked, upset and lost. My tears just kept rolling down my cheeks.

Sunday, 27th December 2009

10th of Muharram, 27th December 2009, Sunday at 8.10 a.m. in the morning Adam departed from this world. He left his mother and everyone else behind. Everyone who loved him dearly, he left in this world regardless of their love. His dad, his brothers and sisters, grandparents, all of his uncles and aunties, his only Phuphie and all of his cousins were shocked and upset when they heard about his death.

By the time my children reached the hospital for the second time, their elder brother, their Adam Bhai (brother), had left this mortal world. They did not have a chance to talk to their brother. Death had taken him away. My children were devastated to look at their brother's body. They too, like me, had not witnessed a death so closely.

Adam's uncle passed his hand over his eyes, and those eyes, which were open and lifeless, were closed. His eyes, with which he saw this world and saw his mother, were closed forever. Those eyes, everyone used to praise. Whenever people met my Adam, the first thing they used to say about him was, "Adam has got very beautiful eyes". He had a rare attraction in his eyes and now those eyes were closed forever.

2. Adam's Funeral

Sunday, 27th December, 2009

After my child left this world I wanted him to be buried as soon as possible. We told the doctor that if we could get the death certificate quickly, we would like him to be buried today.

The doctor said that they could only try, because the offices were closed due to Christmas holidays and the next day, Monday the 28th was a Bank Holiday. But God the most merciful answered my prayer and we got the death certificate promptly.

The nurse removed all the tubes, drips, oxygen mask and everything else from Adam's body, cleaned his body and wrapped him in a white sheet. Then she placed on his chest a card with his name written on it. Even after witnessing everything in front of me, I still could not believe that my child was no more in this world, he had breathed his last breaths, that he will not be able to talk to me and he will never come back.

While still in hospital, I texted the news of his death to my friends and acquaintances. In return, texts and phone calls started to come. All of them were surprised at what had happened, and so suddenly.

I accompanied my son's body into the lift down to the ground floor of the hospital; this was where funeral services' hearses arrive. My father-in-law and Ayub's brothers had all gone home to make arrangements for his burial. Ayub, my children and I also came home and made arrangements for the funeral prayer. I felt like it was my child's Rukhsati[1] (send-off) and I had to see him off on his way.

Some time ago my brother Mohammed had returned from Pakistan. My mother had sent with him prayer cards for a deceased person. She was always sending me Islamic books and literature, but it was the first time that she had sent me this prayer (*du'a*). I was thinking that my mother does not miss to send me anything that I may require in my life, but why would I need this du'a? Even in my wildest dreams, I had never imagined that the prayer she sent me this time would be put to use straightaway. Now I took out those prayer cards.

My brother had also brought a very beautiful cream-coloured georgette dress from Pakistan, which had never been worn. That day I realised that both the dress and prayer cards were for this occasion.

We went straight to the Masjid (Mosque) where the arrangements for the funeral prayer had been made. By the time I reached there, hundreds of people had arrived; family, neighbours, acquaintances and Adam's friends. In the midst of the crowd there were lots of faces I recognised and many whom I did not. I wondered what was going on. Usually, this many people would be seen only at a wedding. People were offering me condolences, women were hugging me and sympathising with me. My thoughts were scattered, my eyes were vacant and my heart was sad. I was in another world all alone by myself in the multitude.

I was watching the people who were in tears. I wondered why they were crying. I am the mother, so why am I not crying?

---

1   *The time/ceremony of a bride leaving her parents' home after marriage.*

Why have they all gathered here?
Have they all come to attend my son's funeral?
Are they all offering me condolence for Adam?
Why are they all so upset?
Has he really left this world?
Will he never come back?
Is it his funeral or his Rukhsati?

Countless questions numbed my mind. Whoever hugged me I hugged them back, whoever said a few words of condolence, I was hearing those, and I was watching people moving from here to there.

It was not long before my child's coffin was brought in; a brown wooden box wrapped in a black sheet with the Kalima written on it. A large number of women had gathered around the coffin. People wanted to see his face. I also came forward, stood very close to the coffin and looked at my child. After getting bathed, my child was wrapped in the sheets which were making his shroud. Adam was sleeping peacefully. He was oblivious to who was around him, who was crying and who was grieving. Peace was written on his face, thanks to God the Almighty.

People were telling me, "Look at his face until your heart's content as you will not get another chance to do so. This is the last time you will be seeing him. You will never be able to see him again." I kept looking at my child with all the strength and courage I could summon.

I gazed upon Adam's face for a long time, trying to imprint this last image of him into my heart. Then I thought that the time for the third daily (*Asr*) prayer was running out, but I was also afraid that they might take the coffin from the women's section to the men's area of the funeral prayer in the mosque.

So I told Farhat (Ayub's sister) that I was going to pray and would be back very soon. Thanks to Allah the coffin was still there when I came back. I spent a little more time with my son, after which it was time for Adam to leave for his funeral prayer. The mourners went away with his coffin after this, and my child then made his journey to the graveyard. Adam was buried before sunset.

I just kept on thinking

I kept thinking that the child who had gone to hospital after sunset last night was buried before sunset today!

Is this how much time it takes for a soul to depart? Adam, who was resting on the sofa yesterday evening watching a football match, was today, the "late Adam Ayub", lying in his grave before sunset this evening. Isn't it strange? I was overwhelmed with the reality of the situation and the power of time! I had never witnessed a death so closely. Now when I had, it was that of a very dear one.

Then I pondered a lot and accepted God's will. I thought of everything associated with Adam's departure that was beneficial for me and my son. I thought deeply and came to the conclusion that this was all God's divine plan and I had no choice, but to accept it. This decision that God has made must be for our good. Whatever He has planned must be best for me.

Yet there were many questions which stormed my mind: What? Why? Why now? How? Any reasons? Advantages and disadvantages?

After much deliberation, I reached the conclusion that I have no reason to complain to Him. I will be considered ungrateful if I do so for many reasons, which I list here.

First of all, I would not usually accompany Adam to the hospital, but on this occasion, I decided to go with Adam on his insistence. Just think for a while what would have happened had I not accompanied him. I would have been devastated.

All praise is due to God alone! It was Him who had put this thought in my child's mind. It was His will that I go with him and watch him dying and departing. Yes, it was painful, but it would have been far worse had I not been there. No matter how much I thank Him for it, it will not be enough.

I am grateful too that my son left home on his feet without being a burden on anyone. Besides a stomachache and a little discomfort in his back, he did not have any cough, fever, cold or breathing problem on our journey to the hospital. All the way he was kissing my hands; he was leaning against me in the car. Whatever God decreed for Adam's suffering was very quick. Adam's condition only worsened once he was on the hospital bed. When he lay there he developed a problem with his breathing.

As much as I grieve losing Adam, I can't thank God enough that He made him suffer the least. God protected my child from pain. All praise due to God who called him back lovingly. No matter how much I thank Him, it will never be sufficient.

I also give thanks that Adam was able to wave goodbye to his Phuphie, grandparents and everyone else. Everybody had reached the hospital in time. Everybody had said goodbye to him. That very day he had talked to his Nani Ammi (maternal grandmother) in Pakistan. He had told her, "Nani Jan! I am not feeling well." It was also on Saturday when he talked to his youngest uncle (father's brother). "I will come to see you on Sunday if I feel better", he told Babur.

All praise is due to God alone that before going he had met people and had spoken with them.

Before leaving our home Adam got to see his brothers and sister, though nobody knew that this was the last time they were seeing one another in familiar surroundings.

It was also a strange coincidence that at Christmas I had taken holidays from work for two weeks to be with the children at home. It had been a long time since we, as a family, we had spent time together. Usually, we do not get much time to be together in our normal daily routines.

Because it was snowing outside, we had all stayed at home, and the last time we were together was at our home on Christmas day.

We were all there at Huma's (my niece) birthday gathering. The last picture of his life and a few moments of video taken there are still preserved. Later, when I looked at that picture, I got scared. In that picture there was no vigour in him. How had I failed to see it?

Our whole family had planned to go together to Bruges (Belgium) for a few days during our two-week break from work. But Adam was feeling lethargic. He said, "I do not want to go, Mum! All of you may go. I will stay with my grandparents".

I do not know what held me back and I said, "Adam, both of us will stay back." Thanks to Allah (SWT), I remained at home and I and my child were given this priceless opportunity to spend precious time together. This was one week before his death.

It was snowing heavily outside on that day too.

The 21st of December was the last time he stayed at his Mamoon's place. We stayed up late that night. He went out with my brother, and they brought back a pizza and a comedy movie. We chatted for quite some time. Who knew that this was the last time Adam would be at my brother's home?

When he got up the next morning he was alright. Auntie Erum had made a Paratha² for him, which he ate.

All praise is due to God alone for the treasured moments I spent with my son. My brother and his wife had returned after staying for three months in Pakistan. It was destined for them to be around during his last days. That is why they had returned. Adam's death could have happened while they were over there, but God had cared for all of us.

Adam's Auntie Zeenat also had planned to go to Pakistan, but she could not get the tickets. Now I think it was God's will that when Adam left this world, all the people who loved him were around him.

We had lovingly renovated our five-bedroom house. Adam had spent one Ramadhan³ and two Eids in this house last year and one Ramadhan and two Eids this year. He lived for one and a half years in this house and left countless memories. I cannot thank God enough that he stayed in this house, in his room and left his fragrance everywhere in our home.

Thanks to Allah (SWT) we do not have any regrets that he did not have a chance to see this house or live in it with us. He has left us with his beautiful memories.

---

2 Homemade flat round bread shallow fried in a pan.
3 A month of the Islamic calendar during which the Muslims observe the fast.

Ayub and myself had taken leave from work for Christmas, and my children's schools were also closed. The schools opened on 4th January 2010. By that time, all the important chores related to Adam's death were completed. Then, it continued snowing and the children's school holidays were extended providing them more time to accept the loss and grieve. Allah (SWT) gave priority to the welfare of my children in every way. All praise is due to Allah alone. No matter how much I thank Him, it will never be enough.

The first night after Adam's death, I was not able to sleep. The thought that my child was in his grave and I was lying on this comfortable bed, in this warm room, in this cold weather, and my child is out there in his grave, was a very strange feeling. I felt very scared and anxious.

The next day someone told me: "God's love for a person is seventy times stronger than that of their mother". So I felt more at ease and realised that my child was not out there in the cold, but he was in God's blessing and I do not have to worry about him. Allah (SWT) will protect my child in his grave. I leave him in God's care and there is no better carer than Him. I also thanked God that I was ritually pure to perform my daily prayers at that time. So I supplicated a lot to Him and prayed to him, which put my heart at peace.

Although it had been snowing, all praise is due to God alone for there was no trouble during Adam's funeral and his burial. It snowed heavier after his burial.

After the first week passed I became very restless, constantly thinking about what had happened last week at this particular day and hour, things the doctors told us; I was reliving all those moments. That very same day Adam's friends came to our place and talked about him. One of them, Lala, had seen Adam in his dream, which he told us about. He told us that Adam was wearing a white robe. There was a lot of light behind him. Adam was saying in his typical style, "Lala, I don't know why they are all so worried about me and missing me! I am very happy here!"

Hearing about this dream put me at peace. I believe the visit of Adam's friends today, and the description of the dream was also God's wisdom and blessing. He wanted to give me solace this way.

I was talking to Farhat till late in the night. The next day was the first Sunday after Adam's death. I thanked Allah that I woke up at 8.30 a.m. in the morning. I thought that Allah (SWT) had saved me from the anguish of getting up earlier because, had that happened, I would have relived all those events from the last Sunday.

There is one graveyard which is closer to our house, but is at a distance from my parents-in-law's home. God in his benevolence made the decision for Adam to be buried in West Bowling graveyard. God also acted fairly here in that this graveyard is in between our place and theirs. And here, Our Lord made another decision in my favour. My sense of direction is not that good. God decided for Adam's grave to be very close to the boundary wall near the main road. In such a vast cemetery, God chose for his burial site to be on one side with an easy approach. I cannot thank him enough.

Day by day, the snowing increased. I heard later that people had trouble digging the grave of someone's child and he could not be buried on time. How can I thank God who made everything related to my son so easy that everything happened effortlessly and well before time.

There are many other incidents which happened in those times where God showed his kindness and benevolence to us. I cannot find the words to thank Allah (SWT) for His blessings.

3. The First Days

Monday, 28th December, 2009

I visited the graveyard for the first time today. When the car entered the graveyard gate, it was a unique experience to witness. There were graves all around. Looking at this scene, I thought about the reality of life in a way I had never felt before.

As the car proceeded inside the graveyard, my thoughts were scattered. I was wondering, which grave my Adam is in? Where is he? Yet, I knew he will not be waiting for me there, he will not be able to talk to me. I will neither be able to touch him nor hug him. I had only come to see a mound of earth which was his last abode.

Suddenly, Ayub stopped the car in front of a grave. The wet earth and the fresh flowers told me that this was my Adam's grave. Also, the gravestone with his name was confirmation that, yes! this indeed was my Adam's grave. I did not have the heart to get out of the car. I just sat in the car and looked at his grave, those flowers, and his gravestone. His name, date of his death, and his age were engraved on that stone.

Initially, I did not have the courage to get out of the car and look closely at my son's burial place. Then I took my inner strength and touched the mud on his grave. I prayed for his forgiveness from God, the most merciful. I wept uncontrollably and then took my leave. Before coming back, I picked up some rosebuds from his grave and brought them home with me and wondered about the fate of flowers.

Some flowers are used to express joy and others are for condolences. Flowers have a deep and a very strong relationship with the human being. When a child is born, people use blooms to reflect their happiness. When he starts a new life at the time of his marriage, the celebration is not complete without flowers, may it be for decorating the stage, or for necklaces or bracelets. There is no better expression of condolence, or indeed any feeling on any occasion, than a bunch of blossoms.

Visiting Adam's grave

The second time I went to the graveyard was on 31st December, the last day of 2009. When Ayub turned the car and entered the graveyard gate, it was as if I knew where my Adam's grave was, although I myself wondered how I remembered it among so many graves because I had been there only once. I felt as though God had told a mother's heart and had consoled her and guided her. Due to heavy snowfall, all the graves were cloaked in white, and there was nothing to identify if it was Adam's grave except his gravestone.

The third time I went to the graveyard was on 10th January. Again it had snowed so much that all the paths were covered with snow. The whole graveyard was deserted. Only the gravestone was there to tell me where my son lay. I was wondering, after someone's death, how would one know who was in which grave except through one's headstone which showed us the whereabouts of the deceased.

I visited for the fourth time on 30th January, but this occasion was different. An auntie (old lady) had died in my neighbourhood. After Adam's death it was the first time that I had looked at someone's face in a coffin. Somebody told me that they had been blessed with a son that day. This forced me to think that Allah (SWT) had created a system. People were entering this world, as well as leaving it, all the time.

1st January 2010
The New Year

Today we all returned from Ammi's place, where we had been staying ever since Adam's passing, to our own. This was not an easy step to take. We spent the whole day at Ammi's, but decided in the evening to go back home; the home where Adam would not be living with us anymore.

Abbu, Farhat and almost all the other extended family members came over to drop us off. We prayed to God and entered the house. The first thing upon opening the door that caught our sight was Adam's shoes. As soon as I stepped inside the room I saw his things were scattered all over the place.

Returning to our own home was a great ordeal. Everybody at Ammi's had consoled us, which had helped with the passing of time, but now there was going to be another test of our patience - how to go through our son's belongings and then either keep them or give them away.

First of all, we prayed to God for peace and His blessings for our home and asked for His forgiveness for Adam. We all had tears in our eyes. We shared the chocolates which my brother had brought for Adam when he had come to visit him that last time. We had never imagined that it would be us who would be eating his chocolates.

The next ordeal was going into his room. We entered it

together. We recited *Surah Yaseen* (36th chapter of Holy Qur'an) and *Surah Mulk* (67th chapter of the Holy Qur'an). We offered the prayers of gratitude to God to have peace in our hearts.

How did I put away his clothes and his belongings?! I can feel that anguish but cannot describe it.

I thought, the New Year has brought something really new for me this year; a life without my firstborn child.

What am I afraid of?

God says, "The bigger the sacrifice I ask for, the greater the reward I will bestow (certainly)". The sacrifice has been made. God has put me through the test, but I am afraid lest there is something which might nullify my deed and my sacrifice, lest I say or do something which God might not approve of.

I pray to God that He will certainly reward me for my patience regarding His Almighty decree and keep me away from any deed which may deprive me of my reward. I have thought a lot about Adam's death, and the only conclusion I can reach was that Our Lord has really put me through a very big test. He wants to see how will I react. This is a test of my faith, my gratitude and my life. I had never taken Adam's health or his illness as a test. I always thought of him as a normal, healthy child, and I never imagined that he could depart because of this illness. In every respect it seems that this is what God has tested me with.

What is it that makes me feel ashamed of myself? Allah has blessed me with so many joys. He gave me ideal parents, the best upbringing, very loving brothers and sister-in-laws, a good husband, such lovely children, good in-laws and best friends. Whatever I wished for in life was fulfilled. Allah (SWT) made everything easy for me. No sufferings at any stage of my life. I always felt that I had Allah (SWT) special blessings upon me. And now that when I am about to turn forty, it is God's will to put me to the test. I am ashamed of myself if I complain. How can I complain to Allah? I feel embarrassed when I think that on one hand there are uncountable blessings and kindnesses of Allah to the utmost, while on the other hand, this sacrifice! Yes, no doubt the sacrifice is not a small one, but taking into account all of His blessings He has given me, this sacrifice did not have to be insignificant.

Allah (SWT) is not unfair. Yes, Adam was my first child and I became a mother by bearing him. Yes, my son was my good friend, and yes, everyone is tearful, but he was Allah's (SWT) choice as well. I submit to His will. Allah (SWT) called my child, His creation, back in such a way that it is hard for me to comprehend.

When I think about his death, it seems like I was holding him like a very fine chinese silk scarf in my hand. God pulled it away so beautifully, lovingly and slowly that He did not let me feel that I was left empty-handed. He saved me from the pain and anguish I might have felt had this scarf been taken away any other way from us. That scarf, no doubt, was God's gift, but thanks to God, He took it back very tenderly. Everything related to Adam happened so swiftly and so well that I was amazed. Every time my thoughts revisit the events of that day, I realise that God did not give me a chance to ponder.

I have submitted to every act of my Creator relating to how and when He called my Adam back. I feel like Allah (SWT) has saved me from a calamity. I do not have the words to thank Him.

It makes me shiver to think:

What if he had had a heart operation and he had passed away during that?
What if he had suffered for a few days in the hospital and I could not bear to see him in pain?
What if he had not insisted on taking me with him?
What if his burial had been delayed?
What if we had not received the Death Certificate in time?
What if they could not dig his grave because of bad weather?
What if that many people could not join his funeral prayer?
What if my children could not reach the hospital in time?
What if he had died at home and had to undergo a post-mortem?
What if...? What if...?

It is such a long list that it sends a chill down my spine thinking about all the What If's. All praise is due to God alone for nothing happened like that. God made everything easier for me, my husband, my children, my family and most of all, for my Adam. Oh Lord! Please forgive me for any insubordination or folly of mine. I ask You for Your benevolence and mercy and ask You to give me endurance, and pray to You for higher places in heaven for my child, Ameen.

Trying to make sense of the unexpected

On the 14th and 15th of December, Adam was in hospital for check-ups of his heart. It was also Ahmad's eleventh birthday on the 15th. Ambar had decided to include Adam's name in Ahmad's birthday card as well.

When we visited Adam in the hospital. I told Ahmad, "We will cut the cake tomorrow when your brother comes home."

Adam sent an "I Love You" text to all of us from hospital. Now I wonder what he had in his mind at that time, because never before had he had done that. Did he know something was going to happen?

The other unexpected thing that happened was that on Eid, Adam said, "Mum, I want to wear a Sherwani on Eid". I was a bit surprised. But I brought a very beautiful Sherwani for him for Eid which he liked very much. It looked as if this Sherwani had been made exclusively for him. He looked very handsome in it when he wore it on Eid. Unfortunately, I do not have any photograph of him in the Sherwani.

During the last few months, I talked a lot to him about his marriage. He knew I wanted him to get married immediately after his degree. "What type of girl would you like to marry, Adam?"

He said to me, "You can start looking for a girl for me." Then he asked, "Are you thinking about any specific girl?"

I replied, "No, but I am asking you to have an idea about what type of girl you prefer."

"Mum! I like Arab girls very much. They are very beautiful," Adam said.

I was very surprised to hear this answer, which was unexpected because he had said this rather than saying that "the girl should be from this country" or "I want to get married in Pakistan".

Now, in retrospect I think these arab girls actually are *Hoors* (maidens in heaven), because this conversation took place a few days before Adam departed. Though I do not know for sure, I have heard the person who is destined to leave this world can have a premonition about it. Having said that, despite these few things, I do not see anything extraordinary. When I think of the Sherwani[1], I feel that God wanted me to see Adam wearing the Sherwani so that a mother should not have any regrets in her heart that she has not seen him in that outfit. All praise is due to Allah alone.

Before his death, Adam shared two of his dreams with me, wherein he saw his own child. Adam was very fond of children, especially toddlers. He would hold them very lovingly. He had experienced this same dream twice where his son was walking with him holding his hand. When I heard that I said, God willing (In Sha Allah), I will witness the happy occasions in your life and see you in a bridegroom's attire".

I always used to tell him, "At the silver jubilee of our wedding anniversary, myself and Dad will be dressed like a bride and a groom and you will attend with your wife. I will invite everyone".

The last three nights of his life in our home, Adam slept in my room. When Dad was on night shift, my son often used to come to my room and we would talk until late. Those last three nights Ayub was on night shift, and because Adam had a stomachache and was being sick, he slept in my bedroom. On those nights we talked a lot. He kissed my hands and said, "Mum, do you know I love you?"

"Yes, my son," I replied. "I know that. I love you, too."

On that final morning at home, Saturday, the 26th, after coming back from his work and offering his prayers, his dad lay beside Adam. I also lay there for a little while. Our child hugged and kissed both of us and went to sleep lying beside

1   Sherwani - A traditional formal dress mostly worn at weddings and special occasions

us. I did not know that this was the last time he was sleeping in this house, in my room, beside his parents.

Now when I view our room and the bed, it feels very strange. To this day, I look at the door of my room thinking that Adam might come in smiling and sit beside me and talk to me.

Adam insisted that I accompany him to hospital. This also makes me wonder; did he know something or had he experienced a premonition, or did he just want me to accompany him? When he left this world, his face was calm and peaceful. He could not tolerate the oxygen mask. Possibly he wanted to leave this world. When Adam looked to his left side and opened and closed his eyes, I felt as if he was going. Angels of death had come to take him away and he was waiting for them.

I had never witnessed death so closely in my life before this. When my grandmother died, I was very young. I cannot remember anything besides a crowd of people and a wooden box. Other deaths I could remember which had shocked me were of my very dear maternal Aunt Bushra and my very loving maternal Uncle Akram which were sudden deaths. They were a brother and sister who were taken to the graveyard together. I came to know about this when I was performing pilgrimage in Makkah (*Umrah*). By the time I reached Pakistan, they had been buried. That too though, was a very vague and remote feeling because I had not witnessed the last moments of their lives. Yet when I was at their place, I had a strong feeling that they might come in through that door, but they never did.

But what I came across in life this time was probably one of the most unique, rare and painful scenes that a mother could experience; witnessing the last moments of her child's life. To watch so closely as he breathed his last breaths. Watching it for the first time and watching the death of my very dear son and friend. None of this was less tormenting than the other.

Allah (SWT) has made this relationship very privileged; the mother and her child's relationship. A woman may forget the loss of every other relative, but losing her child is something she cannot forget, though she may try to do so. I do miss my aunt, uncle, my grandparents and other close relatives who have died, but when Adam left me, only then did I realise that I had never felt this loss before. When people say, "we understand how you feel", they are not telling the truth, because they don't know how you really feel. Only another mother can be aware who herself has suddenly lost her young son and best friend like I did.

Even in his last moments, my son wiped my own and his dad's tears and told us not to cry. Even at that time he was thinking of his parents. He urged us to be patient. Praise is due to God alone for his face was very serene.

4. Closing Chapters

The things Adam often used to say: "You only live once."
Whenever his dad said, "Money doesn't grow on trees", he
used to reply, "Then why do banks have branches, Dad?"

Whenever I said something funny, his response was, "Tell me
when to laugh, Mum."

He used to tease Arslan all the time. "If we both wear the
same clothes and have the same haircut, I will still look ten
times better than Arslan."

He loved his phone. "Dad, I need a contract (mobile phone)
with loads of minutes and a text package, as I have many
friends and every month my minutes finish before the date."

If Ayub and I disagreed about something trivial, he got
irritated and said, "I hate it when you argue about these little
things."

15th January 2011
Death certificate

On the occasion of the birth of each of my children, I went
over to the registry office with Abbu and got them registered.
Now it was Ayub's first visit there, as he and my Father-in-
law went to register Adam's death. They came back holding a
sheet of paper. I had never seen anybody's death certificate in
my life before. The first time, and that, too, of my own child.
I cannot describe how many tears I shed. All praise is due to

God alone that I have never had cause to cry as much as I did then. But somehow I enjoyed shedding those tears.
A poet says:

It seems as if my eyes become fragrant with crying
I can smell the fragrance of your memories in my tears

This piece of paper was confirmation that yes, my child is gone. I was thinking that, now nobody will ever need to look at his birth certificate. Maybe the only official document, if required, will be just this death certificate. How the times and circumstances change.

16th January 2010
How the time passed

How did one week pass? I wondered. How did the second week pass as well? I was upset. It is Sunday today and it has been three whole weeks since my child left this world.

Today is the 16th of January 2010. It is 9:20 am. It is no longer the same year of his death. It is now 2010 instead of 2009. In just three weeks it feels as if Adam had been someone from the past. I experienced the pace of time; how fast it goes. It does not walk, it runs. It runs so fast that I am unable to keep pace with it. It looks like it is running ahead of me and I am trying to catch up to it, but the distance between us is ever increasing. I was getting confused about the time I had spent with Adam and now, a few weeks of him no longer being there. Such a strange mix of feelings I am going through! I cannot determine the time, and I do not understand how recent or distant memories are. I am very confused. I cannot give a name to my feelings.

I am asking myself:

Am I missing him?
Am I restless?
Is it going to be a few weeks since Adam's death?
Did he actually spend 18 years with me?
Is the time passing very quickly or has it stopped?
What is it all about?
Why is it so?
What is happening?
Why am I feeling like that?
Why am I immersed in thoughts?
What is fact and what is fiction?

The 10th of Muharram
The day he left us

> *I can't forget the time when you left*
> *The painful scenes are unforgettable, too.*
> *Your eyelids meeting together are hard to forget;*
> *The funeral, the scene thereof, can't forget it even if I try to*
> *Can't forget how you wiped the tears of your mother*
> *Can't forget how you wiped the tears of your father*
> *(Urfana Ayub)*

My child was called back on such a blessed day. All praise is due to God alone! People yearn for such a day, the 10th of Muharram[1], the Day of the Martyrs, the day my child left this world.

This is another of God's blessings that He chose such a holy

---

1   *A day of great religious significance for the Muslim ,on which many significant events happened and will happen including the date on which the grandson of Prophet Muhammad (Peace Be Upon Him), Hussain (May Allah Be Pleased With Him), was martyred along with his family and friends.*

day for my son. I, of course, will remember, but others will not forget it either and, God willing, more and more people will be able to pray for his forgiveness. It is a special blessing from God bestowed on me and my son. May He forgive all his sins, minor or major, which he committed knowingly or unknowingly? May He have mercy on him and pardon him (Ameen).

By virtue of this book, I will request everyone that if there was any shortcoming in my child's dealings with them, please forgive him. Asking for pardon in this life can save you from punishment in the Hereafter. If you had any lapse in dealing with someone, ask them for pardon and compensate them for it. In the Hereafter, you will be asked very thoroughly about the rights of others. I pray from the bottom of my heart that Allah pardons my child and assigns him a place in a high station in Heaven. As he died on the Day of the Martyrs. (Ameen).

20th January 2010

Today, Ayub and myself went to the University library where Adam had studied, to return the books he had borrowed from there. We also went to see his hospital consultant in Leeds. On the way there, Ayub said, "This might be our last visit to Leeds Hospital with regards to our Adam."

I met Adam's doctor and the senior nurse. They consoled us, and said that if we wanted to ask anything about his death, his last moments or his illness, we could.

Both of us said that we had nothing to ask about. He was destined to leave this world, and this he did.
Then we went to the library, where they also consoled us.

They told us that they had received the news that this student had passed away, and that since they did not expect anybody to come back to return the books, they had ordered new copies of the books. They thanked us for bringing the books back. We went to the University next to meet his course tutor and his personal tutor. Both of them praised Adam a lot. They considered him to be a very hardworking boy, and very cultured as well. He was different from other boys. They showed us the lecture room and the place where he mostly used to sit. They told us that Adam had said in the interview that he was very impressed by his mother. They showed us the letter which they had sent the students to inform them about Adam's death, and they had also altered the timetable a bit to set aside some time to talk about Adam. That letter said that he had died during an operation. We corrected them, explaining what had actually happened.

We met one of his very good friends in university. He was talking about his friend and gave us a picture of himself with Adam that he had meant to give to Adam. Adam had not even had a chance to see this picture, which was taken at an event at the university before the Christmas holidays.

Today I realised that my child had done his share of youth and community work. He left a message for the youth that they should think about their life and the hereafter, spend their lives very carefully and remember God. According to his tutors, had Adam completed his education, he would have been one of the best youth and community workers.

I said, "He had done what he had to; he had spread love. Perhaps he might not have done that much by living in this world compared to what Allah (SWT) made happen by virtue of his death".

Today was a very hard day. I was closing the different chapters of his life which never needed to be opened again. All praise is due to God alone for he did attend the university, and though it was only for a few months, my dream did not remain unfulfilled that he did not attend at all.

Allah (SWT) has not left anything for me to say. How can I complain? I do not have any regrets about my child that he could not do this or that. Allah (SWT) fulfilled every wish of his and gave him the chance to do everything. Very few people can live that rich a life. Allah (SWT) had bestowed His special blessing and kindness on my child. Though Adam's time with us was short, he lived a very beautiful and full life. His life reminds me of a butterfly that has a very brief lifespan, but as long as it lives, it spreads beauty and colour in the world.

Stars in the sky, *As a poet said:*

> *If I look around, everything seems the same*
> *But when I think, there is nothing left after you*

Sitting in the car with the children, I realised that the car is empty. Adam is not in it. When I looked at the sky, I could see Adam's name written there by the stars. I felt as if he is amongst the stars. That is why he is not in my car. He is not amongst us anymore. He is neither in our car, nor our house, not even in this world, but he resides only in our hearts.

Even my heart feels empty without him. "Like a shining star, he is somewhere in the sky." Whenever I look up at the sky, I search for his name there.

In the words of a poet:

Neither are there hurtful memories, nor the throbbing of the heart
As though the heart is broken apart.

21st January 2010

This poem captures my feelings:

I hide all the tears which fall, in my lap
For bare not your heart before others.

Today I desperately wanted to phone Adam knowing very well that he will not be able to answer. I couldn't contain myself and dialled his number. The bell kept ringing, but he did not pick it up. My eyes filled with tears and I cut off the call. When I looked at his mobile phone I saw my missed call.

1 missed call - Mum

Then I tried texting him. I knew his eyes will never read my message but I could not resist and sent a text message to his mobile phone.

"Adam, I love you very much – Mum"

I checked his mobile and read my own message. It was agonising. He could neither pick up my phone nor could he answer my text.

5. Experiences & Memories

Experiences of other people which gave me courage

God gives you patience. Nobody dies with the deceased. If this happened, mothers would have died with their children and children with their mothers. But this is God's system which keeps moving always.

In this regard I remember the example of my maternal aunt and uncle who departed from this world on the same day. I was worried about who would sustain my aunt's family. Her youngest son was very small then, but as time passed, her children grew up. All the children got married. Nothing stopped. It is true that nothing or no one can fill the gap left by a mother, but Allah (SWT) is the only one who gives you the patience and strength to go on.

My maternal uncle also had two small children. He had yearned for children his whole life. When Allah (SWT) blessed him with a son and daughter, he left this mortal world, leaving everyone and everything behind. Both the brother and sister died suddenly. My uncle suffered a heart attack at his sister's funeral and died the same day. Two coffins were taken to the graveyard the same day. This is something that shook up the whole family.

My uncle's children are grown up now. Again, nothing stopped. Life and death go together hand in hand. The world's system keeps moving like it had been. After Adam's death, when I looked around at the people, I came to know of many deaths which helped me understand the actual meaning of death. I was not the only one bereaved; there were many others like me.

A family's daughter, who was the only girl in three generations, was going to be a mother herself for the first time. She suddenly died and went away from this world along with her baby.

Another young girl who was twenty-one years old had some problem with her throat which proved fatal. She died, leaving behind a 4-month-old baby girl.

A lady who was widowed at twenty-nine years of age had eight children, the youngest born two weeks after her husband's death. She struggled her whole life to bring up her children. Recently she discovered she had an advanced stage cancer inside her abdomen.

A couple had seven children. All of them died one after the other. The last daughter died of cancer at seventeen years of age.

A family's parents died in succession. Their children were abroad and could not attend either parent's funeral.

One woman became widowed at twenty-seven years of age. She brought up her children alone without her husband's support.

Another lady got widowed, remarried and got divorced, then married for the third time and became widowed again. Finally, she was widowed for the forth time after another marriage. She died childless after four marriages.

A young girl also got widowed three years after her marriage. She is struggling with her two children.

A man's wife died during the birth of their twin babies. He married again and had two more children. Then he died suddenly, leaving behind a young widow and four children.

A dead body was found. The deceased's identity could not be determined. The body was buried after two days.

A family's only brother died. Six months later, that man's wife also died, leaving six children behind.

A two-year-old child who was suffering from heart disease suddenly fell dead while playing. A post-mortem was done twice and finally the body was handed over to the family after seven days.

A lady went to Pakistan from England to meet her daughter and died there.

Another woman went to Pakistan for her mother's funeral, and during this time her seventeen-year-old son died in England after a severe headache.

A nineteen-year-old boy was murdered. His wife was pregnant. The funeral was held after one month, during which time his wife gave birth to his baby. What can one say about the grief of the mother who lost her son in front of her, the grief of the young widow whose whole future looks bleak and the grief of the newborn baby who was orphaned before his birth?

A family consisting of a mother, father, two sons and a pregnant daughter-in-law had a car accident. During the accident the mother and both sons died. The father and the

49

pregnant daughter-in-law survived. How must their lives have changed?
Those who do not have children yearn for children their whole life.

I met an old lady, (*Amman ji*) in the Prophet's Mosque (*Masjid Nabawi*), She told me she was blessed with nine sons after having two daughters. Eight of those children died at different ages. Only one survived who got married and had five children. He also died at the age of fifty years. The old lady's husband died, too. Now she is living with her daughter-in-law and five grand-children. After so many calamities, she is still alive at 90.

These are not just stories. These are real happenings in the lives of real people. There are numerous other stories which I have heard, but could not write about. All of these gave me so much courage and strength that my own grief seemed small in comparison.

All praise is due to God alone for Adam was not my only son. Allah (SWT) has blessed me with two more sons and a daughter. I cannot thank Him enough. I am not a widow. May God bless my husband with a long life (Ameen). I can never be grateful enough for these bounties. I am not disabled. All thanks is due to God alone. God has graced me with uncountable blessings in my life. I can never thank Him enough. I am surrounded by people who love me, All praise is due to Allah alone.

Adam's habits and daily routines that I will never forget

Adam used to put cream on his hands in the morning before going to the university. After putting the cream in the cupboard, he shut the door with a bang. I always told him to close the door gently and chided him by saying, "You can bang it because it is not going to cost you anything." He used to smile in return.

Whenever he went out or came back home, he would come to me and hug me. Before going to sleep at night, he'd come up to our room and kiss his father and me goodnight.

He would always ask me, "How am I looking, Mum?", with a big smile on his face. I never praised him wholeheartedly. Instead, I just said, "You're looking fine."

Whenever he had to go out with friends, Adam would say, "I'm going out, Mum", and I always replied, "Are you asking me or telling me?"

In the meantime, one of his friends would arrive and be waiting outside. Adam would leave, laughing and saying, "My friend is here. I'll tell you when I come back."

Jokingly, I would threaten to tell him off upon his return. His usual answer was, "I love you, Mum", and off he'd run.

When he went out in the evening with friends, I asked him, "If you're planning to go to the club, take me with you so that I can also see what happens there."

Adam always laughed and answered, "Mum do you think I will go to such a place?!"

We used to joke like this regularly. Often he'd hug me and say, "I love you, Mum."

Adam was learning to drive. When we were returning home from somewhere and stopped at a shop close to the house to buy roti (bread cooked from unleavened dough), he liked asking if he could drive the rest of the way home. He would plead with me and I would always refuse. In fact, I even pretended that I did not hear him.

Sometimes, he would get angry and say, "Mum, you know I can drive. We are so close to home, why don't you let me drive?"

My answer was always the same: "You can drive once you pass your driving test. It's better to take caution."

Whenever Adam went to his room after taking a bath, he would take a cotton bud from my room to clean his ears. There were always cotton buds in my dustbin.

Adam had a habit of swiping his finger a few times on his nose and smiling. If he tried to hide something, he'd always say, "I'll tell you later, Mum."

The Ramadhan of 2009
A strange coincidence

A few months before Adam's death, on the 27th night of Ramadhan, Ayub, the children and I went to the Masjid for prayers. I met a lady there who asked me about Adam. I did not recognise her. I replied, "All praise is due to God alone, Adam is fine, but excuse me, I do not recognise you."

She reminded me that when Adam had undergone a heart operation at five years of age, her son also had surgery in the same hospital. So I asked about her son. She replied, "My son died two years back. He died in 2007 when he was fourteen years old." The emotions I felt on hearing this were such that I had never experienced before.

I offered my daily obligatory prayer (*salah*) with more devotion than I had never offered before in my life. Tears kept shedding unceasingly from my eyes. They were tears of thankfulness, of humility, of God's grace and kindness. I thanked God that night with all my heart. I realised that God's special blessings were with me. The test which He had put that lady through; He could also have put me through the same. But thanks to God, my son was eighteen years old now and living a full life.

I remained tense and apprehensive the whole day. To Allah alone belongs absolute power. It could have been my child instead of hers who died. Allah took away her son and my son is still with me. God granted life to my Adam.

Now that Adam is no more, I have given a lot of thought to this incident. It is a strange coincidence that I had never come across that lady in so many years. Then she suddenly met me just a few months before Adam's death during Ramadhan and told me the news of her son's death. This made me greatly conscious of the fact that my son could also have been taken away. A mother's son was taken from her, but not mine, though the chances of my son's death were similar to this woman's child. There must be God's wisdom in all this. Then a few months later my Adam died. Next 27th of Ramadhan it will be about one year since his death.

It seems to me that Allah gave me a sign, by making me meet that woman. A clue that my son can also be returned; a forewarning. Her son was fourteen years old when he went back to his Creator. All praise is due to God alone for He gave me four additional years to spend with my son. I cannot thank Him enough. My child spread happiness and filled my life with beautiful memories before going, All praise is due to God alone.

25th January 2010

Adam's phone rang at 9:00 this morning. It was actually a reminder of "Back at University", as the university was due to open today after the Christmas holidays. I thought that tomorrow it will be a full four weeks since his departure from this world. Similarly, there was also a reminder on 4th January, because Adam had to submit his assignment then. This was the first assignment he had started working on before his death, for which he had borrowed books from the library.

On the 22nd I received a letter from Specsavers Opticians reminding Adam to have his eyesight tested because it was two years since his last check-up. They asked him to get an appointment. These letters were causing so much anguish to me. What eye test? The eyes which had shut forever? The eyes which my eyes could no longer gaze upon? Adam also had an appointment with the heart consultant on 20th January.

Today I received Arslan's National Insurance number card in the post. This reminded me that Arslan will be sixteen in March God willing (In Sha Allah). Then suddenly I remembered the time when Adam's card had come. When Adam went to college I felt elated that my son was old enough to be an adult.

While sitting in my room at night...

I most acutely feel Adam's absence when I sit in my room at night. He always used to come to my room and sit and talk with me. He always hugged me before going up to his own room. My eyes became tearful. May God give me strength (Ameen).

As a poet describes:

> *After you left, despite my struggle to control them*
> *My eyes keep crying repeatedly even up to this day.*

I remember him saying, "Mum, I want cheese on toast," in the morning. I always asked if I should make two toasts and every time, he used to answer, "I want only one."

It was my daily routine to take the children out in the morning and drop them off to their schools one by one. In the end only Adam and I would be left. We had a little chat before I dropped him at the bus stop or near his grandmother's house and I went to the office myself.

But now this does not happen and won't happen ever again. Nobody will ask for "cheese on toast" in the morning and there will be nobody sitting with me in the car after leaving the children to school.

May Allah (SWT) place my son in the highest station in Heaven and may He give perseverance to us (Ameen).

A Mu'min's (believer's) life is like a star

I read somewhere that a believer's life is like a star that leaves behind light after completing its lifespan; the light that guides and benefits others. I could not help thinking that my son's life was also like that.

When a flower blooms, its fragrance perfumes the whole garden. Like a single candle that burns, it lights the whole room by its radiance.

When I think in these terms, I feel strengthened. I also take comfort in a poet's words:

He has gone back to his house, do not mourn him
That long was he to be here, do not mourn him

6. The Bitter Truth of Life

27th January 2010

It is one month since Adam left us. Time was flying and I was watching it, helpless and powerless. My heart was desolate. How I wished he would come from somewhere and hug me and I could keep looking at him.

Today I received a condolence letter from the governor of his university. He had praised Adam's character and behaviour and expressed his commiseration. I wept bitterly on receiving the letter. These little bits of paper are proof that my son indeed came into this world and is gone now.

As a poet said:

> *All the seasons passed by, and I remembered the dream*
> *I remember the moment in which the centuries passed by*
> *His voice had all the seven colours of the rainbow*
> *I forgot the whole gathering; only his face remained in my mind.*

30th January 2010

Today I received a condolence card from the university in which Adam's classmates had written their comments. I went to his grave today.

There, I remembered a poet's words:

I cannot forget your memories – no, I can't
They are the only souvenirs of you left with me.

The only support for me is your memories, and all praise is due to God alone what a strong support that is! I can spend the rest of my life on this support. They are the last reminders of you which I will cherish forever, reminders for which I do not need to open any album or to look at any of your belongings. These memories have become a part of my being.

These verses sum it up:

Incidents come and pass by
Memories live with us forever.

4th February 2010
Passport

Ayub had sent Adam's passport to the passport office, which they returned to us today. They had cut its corners because it is of no use to anybody now. No one will carry this passport, nor will it ever be needed for travel purposes again. Yet this is more proof for us that Adam was our son. This is his passport, his reminder. The stamps on the passport will keep reminding us of the places he had travelled to.

There was a condolence letter with the passport as well. The expiry date on the passport was in 2012, but the person to whom the passport belonged expired earlier than that.

12th February 2010

After Adam's death, this was the first night that Ayub returned to working the night shift. The whole family supported me. Farhat, Tayyaba (my cousin), my nephews and nieces all came to stay with me. Everybody felt Adam's absence.

13th February 2010

It was the first night I spent alone with my three children. Adam's absence confuses me and I think:

Is he in this world? Or is he not?
If he is in this world, why can't we see him?
Has he gone somewhere?

It gave me a chance to meditate about life and death. I pray to Allah (SWT) that this meditation and analysis remain a part of my life forever (Ameen), so I continue benefitting from this experience.

Today, on some friends' insistence, I went to a friend's get-together for the first time after Adam's death. I felt very lonely. The world seemed different, empty. I felt like a stranger in the gathering.

As Tayyaba said:

> *We have to accept the bitter truth of life*
> *We have to accept that a person has left us forever*
> *He will not return even if we call him hundreds of times*
> *We have to smile for others, though the heart is crying*
> *(Tayyaba Kanwal)*

17th February 2010

Today I had to go to a friend's place for condolence. Adam's graveyard was on the way. It was evening time. I cannot describe in words what I felt when my car passed through the main road of the graveyard. I felt that I am powerless. I am passing through this road, but my child is here. How can I leave him here? Am I being disloyal to him? People are afraid of ever entering a graveyard at night.

How many times will I pass through this road and endure the feeling of helplessness coming over me? I had to reason that I must accept the fact that my child will never come home with me now. The final abode of every human is indeed a grave. It is Adam's home now, too.

This realisation shocks me to the core. I feel and accept the fact that I am very helpless and powerless. At the same time, I am aware of God's might, power and His benevolence. Undoubtedly, He has power over everything.

19th February 2010

I invited the family to my place so that we could all pray for Adam's forgiveness. Everyone was gathered at our house but my eyes were looking for my son. When my father-in-law Abbu Ji referred to him as "the late Adam" during supplication (*dua'a*), I felt the pain of his going away very acutely, ripping open the deep wound within me.

22nd February 2010

Today I went back to work for the first time after Adam. Life's routine had begun once again, but I felt as if I was in some other place. Although it was the same building and same people, my perception and sensation had altered a lot. The outside world was the same as ever. I took my son's framed photograph with me to my office and placed it on the desk in front of me. It seemed like he was looking at me. I could not concentrate on the office work and left for home.

27th February 2010

It is exactly two months since Adam died. Time is passing. The first month passed very swiftly. The second one seemed as if it has stopped moving, but today even that has passed. Now the time span has moved beyond days and weeks and has gone into months. When twelve months go by, the measurement would move from months to years. In two months' time the date 27th has moved from Sunday to Saturday. Every Saturday and Sunday leaves me mournful. Every 27th date leaves me sorrowful.

Like a poet said:

Afflictions come and go
People remain the same - only their circumstances change.

7. Mother's Day

1st March 2010

Today I had a very strong feeling that Adam's passing away has left me at a strange turn in life. There are many people who are of the opinion that what had to happen, did happen. Enough time was given to mourn the deceased and appropriate condolences were also offered. Now everything should go back to normal. I was quite surprised at this attitude. Different people react divergently to happiness and sorrow. Like on a joyous occasion, some people thank God and offer prayers of gratitude to Him, while others express their happiness by partying and celebration. The former donate money to charity and the latter spend it in a spendthrift manner.

Every person has a different psyche and mindset. If one of our most prized possessions is broken or a precious ring is lost, we brood over it the whole day even though it was a non-living thing. If we remove a framed picture from a wall where it was hanging for some years, that wall seems empty and barren. The desolation of the empty wall reminds us of the frame every time we happen to look at it.

My child was a living human being; God's most superior creation. He was a part of my being that is lost somewhere now. I am aware of the vacuum it has left inside me. He walked this very earth and talked. He was a very good friend of mine. The agony of losing him is undoubtedly the worst of the agonies in my life. I can never forget him and neither do I want to forget him. I only pray to God to grant me patience to bear this loss and to never allow me forget him. The heartache and pain associated with his memories also keeps me connected to God and I want this connection to become stronger with each passing day (Ameen).

Today again Adam was in my memories. I wanted to cry my heart out. There is an uncanny emptiness around me. This emptiness is inside my being and outside as well. It is confusing knowing that he is with us no more but is in his grave.

A prayer to Allah (SWT)

I pray to my Lord to preserve forever the pain and anguish which he has given me so that my faith remains strong and unfaltering. This sorrow rekindles my faith. The more I grieve, the more I will remember God and the more I will understand the reality of this world.

I never want these wounds to heal. I wish that God always keeps my eyes wet with tears because of Adam's memory and because of God's love and awe. May He keep my heart knowing and conscious so that sensitivity is preserved and perception is life.

This heartache has become more precious to me than anything on this earth. I had heard people cherish their sorrows. I used to wonder how sorrows can be endured. Now, I know!

Perception

Your perception is pleasant
Your character is perfect
There is fragrance in your etiquette
And joy in your being

Your heart is like a river
You are unequalled
No matter how much I loved you
But could not hold you back
As if the wind carrying fragrance has stopped
This is my perception of your departure.

(Urfana Ayub)

4th March 2010

This morning I received a recorded delivery. When I opened the door, the postman gave me a card. It was a condolence card from the staff at Adam's primary school where he completed his nursery and a few years of schooling. There are still a few teachers in this school who had taught Adam. It felt good to know that they still remembered him and talked about his childhood in kind words. They also apologised that it took them some time to find my new address. After a while, Interflora delivered the flowers sent by the school. This brought back his memories. The whole day I kept reminiscing about his nursery days when he used to go there with his Baba.

I made up my mind to go to his school and thank everyone, so as to close this chapter forever, just like I had closed the chapters of his college, university, doctor and dentist.

9th March 2010

Today, for the first time, I wished to go to the graveyard alone. Though it was difficult, something was compelling me to go there. I knew I had to do this and I knew I had to do it alone.

I went to the cemetery during the daytime. There were only

a few people there. Some labourers were cutting the trees and very few people could be seen around. The graveyard was mostly deserted. I could not help thinking that the world outside the graveyard gate was so very different from the one inside.

The outside world was least concerned with the preparations for the inside world. All the activities and endeavours were for the outside world only.

Our looking for employment, being engaged in business, doing two jobs a day, building houses and buying cars; all of this is for the outside world. Even our hurriedly offered prayers, during which our mind wanders off to the problems of this world, or maybe the good deeds which we do, are all for our hereafter.

All praise is due to Allah alone, today I believe that I have developed a new relationship with this graveyard and my son's grave, a relationship which had not been formed until now. On previous visits, when I have come here and looked at the gravestone where my son's name is written, it seemed that there was always something missing. Today, I felt as if that desire had been filled.

It is also by God's grace that, due to my child, I have come to see the graveyard as the most significant and truthful place; a place of forewarning and caution for everyone.

"I love you, Adam." Mum

I noticed a poem written on a grave that depicts my emotions.

Another month, another year

Another smile, another tear
Another summer, winter too
But there, never will be Another
You (ADAM)

(Unknown writer)

Sunday 14th March 2010
Mother's Day

Today was Mother's Day. I kept thinking of Adam and the previous year when all of my four children were with me. I took out my "Mum Jewellery" which my children had presented to me last year, and I wore it. Adam had given me an inscribed bracelet. I put that on, too. Ayub and I went to the graveyard and prayed for Adam.

Today my sister-in-law, Farhat, came to visit me. Instead of Adam, she gave me a gift for mother's day. She also gave me a very pretty card, which I believe Adam, if he had gone to buy a card, would also have selected. The message written inside was also very beautiful and special.

When Adam died, I gave cards to everybody on Adam's behalf. What he would have written if he had had the chance to say goodbye? I wrote messages on cards and gave them as gifts. I knew that Adam would never write to me now, but Farhat's gesture of presenting me with a card on Adam's behalf really touched me. I could not hold back my tears.

I remembered the card Adam gave me the previous year and the words he had written on it. I could never have known then that would be Adam's last message to me.

"Mum, you are the only one that I could dream of having. I

hope you have a really great life and wish you do the things you have dreamed of. I LOVE YOU so much that this world cannot fill the space of our mother-son friendship." ADAM

16th March 2010

Today, my sister-in-law Erum, my brother and their children came to visit us. Erum and Mohammed said they would help me to clean the garden. Ever since Adam had died, I have not gone out into the garden much.

Whilst Erum was cleaning, she suddenly came to me and said, "Baji (title used to address an elder sister or any woman a few years older than oneself), do you know Adam's name is written on the ground?" I accompanied her and saw my son's name, ADAM, written near the wall in our garden. My eyes filled with tears and that day flashed through my memory when Adam had written his name in wet cement.

Adam's name written in the house in his own handwriting became another souvenir that he left behind. Like so many other things, I could never have known that his name inscribed on the floor would become memorable for all of us.

Life is so strange. We do not give due credit to all that we possess. Now I think we should value the people around us much more; who knows when they will go away? Just like my Adam went away so suddenly.

24th March 2010

I met Adam last night in my dream. During the dream, I was aware that he had gone. He was looking about 16 years of age.

He did not appear surprised. He looked just normal. I touched his face. I kept calling his name and weeping at the same time knowing that my child has died.

When I woke up I was sobbing. I looked all around me. There was nobody there. My dream was over and my son was nowhere around. My face was wet with tears and my heart was beating wildly. I tried to convince myself that what I saw was only a dream and not reality. The only place where I can meet Adam before my own death was in dreams. I remained restless the whole day.

As a poet said:

Everything changes when your dear ones go away yes, your style of living also changes
It is true one does not die because of separation but may Allah (SWT) never separate dear ones.
Ameen

8. Consolations and Coincidences

27th March 2010

Today it is exactly three months since Adam went away. Every Saturday and the 27th of each month makes me sad. I took my son to hospital on a Saturday and he left this world on the 27th.

Arslan turned 16 today, and I was forced to think that if the 27th brought sorrow for me, it has brought happiness too. Adam went away on the 27th and my Arslan came into this world on the same date.

This fact has taught me that days, dates and times are not bad per se. It is the various incidents and experiences which happen on these days and dates which make them happy or sorrowful. Nothing is bound to these days and dates. Everything is the power of God.

All the children from our entire family came together at my house, but my eyes were seeking Adam in the gathering.

Like a poet says:

> *Searching you on the endless roads of memories*
> *I wither away every day like autumn leaves.*

We all prayed for Adam's forgiveness and for Arslan's health, as well as his conviction in Allah and Islam and prosperity in this world and the Hereafter. I hugged and caressed Arslan.

3rd April 2010

Ammi had lovingly preserved Adam's first baby suit. It was yellow. Later, she gave it to me. And, some time before his death, Adam had bought a black jacket which he wore to the hospital. Now I took out both these things. When I hugged the soft babygrow it seemed as if I was hugging my son. When I looked at it with my tearful eyes, the suit was empty. I thought of the day when I had brought baby Adam home from the hospital. Everyone was so happy. There was a smile on every face. This tiny baby had brought joy to the whole family. He was loved and cherished by everyone.

In the words of a poet:

> *How can I even think about forgetting you?*
> *Closely knit is my each breath with your memories.*

I hugged the black jacket which Adam wore to the hospital. I breathed in the fragrance in the jacket and cried.

There is one puzzling dilemma that often confuses me. It has been only three months since Adam left us, but sometimes I feel as if he never came into this world. Why were the memories of the time he spent in this world fading out so quickly?

Besides this dilemma, there were many other questions, to which I could find no answers. I feel my eyes also bow before Allah (SWT). The tears that fall from them take me closer to Allah (SWT) and wash out the misunderstandings and dust from my heart. It seems as if Allah is telling me, "This is life's reality". One has to accept that. If I do not understand it even now, it will be my own loss.

I also believe that this is God's will and system that the love and memories of people who go away from this world gradually fade out from our minds so that we can begin to live again.

When I think and yearn for my son, it feels as if I will suffocate; as if I will not be able to take another breath. My heart despairs, but then with God's grace I get over these feelings and thank Him.

17th April 2010

This evening, during my qur'an class, the lady sitting next to me asked, "I have heard that one of our classmate's sons, who was a teenager, suddenly died. Do you know her?"

I answered, "Yes, I am the one. My son died suddenly."

That woman consoled me and said longingly, "I cannot understand your grief. I do not have children. I have yearned for children my whole life, but your sorrow is much greater than mine. When Allah (SWT) blesses you with children and they grow up, the pain of their loss is heart breaking. May Allah give you patience."

I thanked Allah in my heart. I am not childless, nor was Adam my only son. Praise be to Allah (SWT), for He has blessed me with three more healthy children.

18th April 2010

Today was my niece Hina's eighteenth birthday. All the children in the family were gathered, but my eyes were looking for Adam on the sofa in Auntie Raheela and Uncle Basat's house where he used to sit. Incidents like these make me cry uncontrollably. My eyes keep seeking my child and my heart is desolate. I long to see him, meet him. It makes me very restless.

The world seems a very different place now.
My life's aim has changed!
The world of my heart has changed since he left
This world has become a desolate place since he left.

(Urfana Ayub)

19th April 2010

I went shopping and saw a frame with the words "I love Mum" written on it. Suddenly, Adam's last few words which he had written for me on the mother's day card flashed before my eyes.

I bought that frame thinking that it was given to me by Adam. I framed his writing in it. May Allah grant forgiveness to my child (Ameen). My son, I love you, too.

9. Ayub Goes to Hospital

20th April 2010

Ayub was not feeling well today. He asked me to bring a pen and a paper. He wanted to say something important to me. "If I am no more in this world, do such and such things in such a way after me. The feeling that I may die suddenly is also a result of Adam's departure."

Our son's sudden passing has evoked this feeling of "be ready" in us a feeling that probably was not so intense before.

21st April 2010

I went to Adam's primary school to give them a Thank You card. The school's building had changed considerably. Quite a lot of construction and renovation work was still going on. Adam had enjoyed good years in this school and he took with him many fond memories of it.

I met one of his childhood teachers. She could understand my pain since she had also lost her twenty-two-year-old son in an accident.

Today, this chapter also was closed forever.

26th April 2010

Ayub suddenly felt unwell. His breathing became troubled. He turned pale and his whole body became cold. I rushed him to hospital where they put an oxygen mask on him. Seeing Ayub wearing the mask brought back memories of Adam. All those same tests were being carried out again, and finally, the long wait for the result of his lung scan.

The medical team were concerned that fluid had collected in his lungs. I could hardly believe we were reliving such a similar scene. Adam's face was in front of my eyes this whole time. Ayub, too, had tears in his eyes.

The results of Ayub's tests showed that there were blood clots in his lungs, which could have been quite serious if immediate medical intervention had not taken place. Thanks to God, his problem was diagnosed in time and appropriate treatment was started promptly.

But the first twenty-four hours were critical. Ayub was kept in a coronary care ward where he could be constantly monitored.

The next day he was moved to an ordinary ward.

27th April 2010
New beginning

Today it is as if I received a sign from Allah (SWT) to live the life that one has been given and be thankful to Him. The one who was destined to go has gone. Be mindful of all those bounties from Allah which you still possess.

This very sign became all the more important because the doctors said, "This man is lucky to have survived with so many clots on the lungs. It is difficult to save a patient's life in such cases."

When clots form in the lungs, breathing becomes very difficult and it is the breathing which keeps us alive. The moment breathing stops, life ends.

On this day, four months have passed since Adam's death. Allah has given a new life to Ayub, All praise be to Allah (SWT).

As Tayyaba said:

You do not gain anything by crying in the night of loneliness
You do not gain anything by building a house on a seashore
After losing him I kept yearning to find him
You will not gain anything by drawing a circle on water.

(Tayyaba Kanwal)

28th April 2010

After visiting Ayub, as I was leaving the hospital and going towards my car, someone called out to me from behind. "You are Adam's mother, aren't you?"

I turned around to find an old acquaintance of mine. Her son used to go to school with Adam in primary school. I was experiencing mixed emotions because someone had recognised and addressed me by referring to Adam. I realised that, although he was gone, people often called parents through their child's reference. It was good to hear myself being referred to as "Adam's mother", but...

75

When I replied, "Yes, I am Adam's mother," she told me about her son and asked me about Adam. I felt very sad when I told her that Adam was no longer amongst us. She consoled me. Her son was also studying in the same university where Adam used to go. I remained depressed the whole day. His memories kept nagging me.

29th April 2010

Today is Thursday, and Ayub is still recovering in the hospital. Ever since Adam has gone, his friends have become Ayub's friends. Adam connected us with many new people before leaving.

Today, four of Adam's friends came to visit Ayub. His face lit up on meeting them. When he meets Adam's friends, they talk to Ayub about football, the game that Adam liked so much. It took quite an effort to keep my emotions under control. My tears flowed as though they would not stop.

As a poet said:
> *It's a long period since we parted,*
> *Still, that person has not gone out of my sight*

I felt a strange longing in my heart when I saw these teenagers talking to Ayub. We did not know these boys. They were not Ayub's friends. They were our son's friends and at this moment the very person who was responsible for our meeting them was not in our midst.

Adam had left behind a big void. If only he was also present here sitting among his friends and talking to his dad. If only! May God place my child in the highest level of heaven and may He pardon all his sins (Ameen).

Adam's Photos

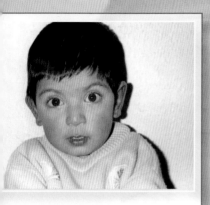

1993, Adam (Age 2)

1994, Adam (Age 3)

1997, Adam (Age 6)
ith younger brother Arslan (Age 3)

1996, Adam (Age 5)
With younger brother Arslan (Age 2)

1996, Adam (Age 5)
With younger brother Arslan (Age 2)

1998, Adam (Age 7)
With younger brother Arslan (Age 4)

2001, Adam (Age 10)

2000 Adam (Age 9)
With younger brothers Arslan (Age 6
Ahmed (Age 2)

2007, Adam (Age 16)

2007, Adam (Age 16)

2007, Adam (Age 17)

2007, Adam (Age 16)
With younger brother Arslan (Age 13)

2007 Adam (Age 18)
With younger brothers Arslan (Age 15) Ahmed (Age 10)

As the poet said:
This life has two parts
This life and hereafter
Between these two there is a distance of only breath.
If breathing, then this life
If breathing stops then other life.

10. Adam's Birthday

7th May 2010, Friday

I wanted this day to become memorable for me. I did not want to spend the day crying. On the contrary, I wanted to spend it amidst fond and loving memories and with my near and dear ones who had always supported me. I asked everyone to dress up nicely and come to my house with joy. This was a day to thank God, not to sympathise or grieve together.

Today my son Adam turned nineteen. This was his day. I put up a brave show without Adam. I wore pretty clothes and looked my best. While I was cooking, I kept thinking that everyone was coming to my house for my child. But suddenly, the realisation struck me. "Where is my son?" I felt upset.

Won't he participate in his birthday? When all the guests arrived, my eyes kept looking for Adam. How I wished he were here, too. I had put away all his photographs. I wanted to see his face, but could not muster up the courage. We all prayed for the highest rewards for him in the hereafter.

Farhat gave me a surprise gift on everyone's behalf. It was a beautiful present; maybe the best gift of all.

Two large album files containing poems, messages, letters, cards, and most of all, much love from all the relatives and friends. I will treasure them all my life, God willing. They contain everyone's affection, Adam's memories and many prayers.

On the whole, the day was a pleasant one.

Reading those messages, letters and cards made me cry. At the same time, I thanked Allah (SWT) that my son was dearly loved by everyone. He gathered so much love before going. Not everyone is so lucky.

All praise be to God, in his short life, he found the love, respect and status of a long lifetime. It was God's special gift that he was blessed with the best character and no doubt, his smile was a gift to him also from God. I am thankful to Him that people always remember and talk about my son fondly.

15th May 2010

I woke up early today missing Adam. I heard a song from an Indian film called Three Idiots on the radio. It seemed to me as if it was written especially for Adam. Every word of the song expressed Adam's habits and ways. My heart was heavy with Adam's memories and I cried throughout the song.

He was like blowing wind
He was like a flying kite
Where can I find him?
We were moved by destiny
He fashioned his own destiny
He fell, got up and walked happily
While we worried about tomorrow
He used to celebrate today
He lived each moment fully
He was like a shade in the scorching sun
He was like an oasis in the desert
He was like medicine for the wounded heart

We used to be afraid in the well While he dived in the stream
He would swim against the tide
He was like a stray cloud
He was very dear to us
Where can I find him?
Where did he come from?
He touched our heart
Where can I find him?

(Music: Shanta Nomolra. Singer: Shan-2009)

21st May 2010

I received the results from a recent blood test today. I had rickets (vitamin D deficiency). The doctor prescribed the same tablets for me that Adam used to take. After Adam died, I had put all his medication in my car to return them to the pharmacy, but they were still lying in my car. When the doctor prescribed those tablets for me, I got them out of the car and used my son's medicine.

As they say, each morsel of food bears the name of the one who is to eat it. Maybe these tablets bore my name and not Adam's.

22nd May 2010

We had been thinking of planting fruit trees in our garden for quite some time. Today, we planted nine trees of apples, pears, peaches, plums and other fruits. I prayed that God may make them grow and produce fruit. Whenever we eat their bounty, we will think of Adam because we had planted all the trees in Adam's memory.

26th May 2010

I went to another graveyard in Bradford. Every time I used to pass by that graveyard, I used to think of going in. While passing through it, I came across a new grave. The word "SON" was written on it in fresh flowers.

It was the final resting place of someone's twenty-three-year-old son who was buried on 21st May. There were a lot of people in the graveyard. Most of the graves were of Muslims. I feel as if I enjoy being in a graveyard. I am tired of gatherings. I feel very lonely.

27th May 2010

Five months have passed!
Don't ask me how they have passed. Both the perceptions go hand in hand. Perception of time passing in the blink of an eye! And the perception of centuries passing by!

I have become very sensitive. Many days have passed since I met Adam in my dreams. How quickly the days turn into months and soon these months will turn into years.

I can never be the old Urfana again, but I am pleased this new Urfana enjoys a higher status than the old Urfana, because she is more aware of and concerned for the hereafter. Now I want to reach there quickly. I have to meet my son; he is waiting for me...

I am not afraid of meeting Allah (SWT). I only wish Allah allows me the time to make preparations for meeting Him.

29th May 2010

Zain Bhikha, the well-known nasheed singer, and his friends had a show in Bradford today. I went there with Ayub, Farhat and the children. It was an impressive performance. Five months back I had not even heard of his name.

Someone had sent one of his nasheeds, 'Allah Knows', on Adam's death and a friend presented me with one of his albums. Since then, I have developed a strong connection with this nasheed.

While sitting in the hall listening to the programme, I thought I had never planned to see his performance. But Zain Bhikha's nasheed now has such a powerful association with me and my son's death that I simply had to come.

The lyrics of this nasheed are so moving that everyone can feel its relevance to their lives in some way. The words also bring solace, in that no matter what difficulty or pain you are experiencing, whether trivial or big, "Allah knows" everything. Nothing is hidden from Him. Our problems, our tears; nothing is hidden from Him. He knows everything.

Allah Knows

When you feel all alone in this world And there's nobody to count your tears Just remember, no matter where you are Allah knows
Allah knows
When you're carrying a monster load And you wonder how far you can go
With every step on that road that you take Allah knows
Allah knows

CHORUS

No matter what, inside or out There's one thing of which there's no doubt
Allah knows Allah knows
And whatever lies in the heavens and the earth Every star in this whole universe
Allah knows Allah knows
When you find that special someone Feel your whole life has barely begun
You can walk on the moon, shout it to everyone Allah knows Allah knows
When you gaze with love in your eyes Catch a glimpse of Paradise
And you see your child take the first breath of life Allah knows Allah knows

CHORUS

When you lose someone close to your heart See your whole world fall apart
And you try to go on but it seems so hard Allah knows Allah knows
You see we all have a path to choose Through the valleys and hills we go
With the ups and the downs, never fret, never frown Allah knows Allah knows CHORUS (x2)

BRIDGE:

Every grain of sand
In every desert land, He knows Every shade of palm,
Every closed hand, He knows Every sparkling tear,
On every eyelash, He knows.
Every thought I have,
And every word I share, He knows Allah knows.

(Zain Bhikha)

14th June 2010

Today, I went to the graveyard alone. I have developed an unusual but powerful and beautiful association with my son's grave.

In the words of a poet:

> *The face which had found abode in my eyes*
> *Remained constrained in my tears my whole life.*

I cried my heart out. I prayed for Adam's forgiveness and patience for myself, after which I finally calmed down and relaxed. Every time I come here, I realise how quiet and serene this place is. I find comfort here. I want to visit this place. I have been living in this country for the last twenty years, but I never had a chance to go to a graveyard.

All praise due to Allah (SWT). Thank you to my son, who has brought me to the graveyard.

24th June 2010

My work colleagues have supported and stood by me during these trying times. I invited them to my home to thank them. Whilst preparing food for them, I suddenly realised why I had invited them, and I answered myself. To thank them. For what? And again, the connection was Adam.

When I think about him, I become restless and depressed. Then I pray to Allah (SWT) for patience and endurance.

As the poet says:

The pain makes me sorrowful, no doubt I know it is not going to go away.
But this is my relation with my Creator. I only pray that He grants me tolerance to bear it.

Undoubtedly, there is no reward better then patience and forbearance. I do not want to get involved in the festivities of this world. His grave is always in my thoughts and his smiling face before my eyes.

27th June 2010
Six months

The date is the 27th again and the day is Sunday as well. When I glanced at the clock, the time was also the same. Ten minutes past (8:10 a.m.). Since Adam went away, the days turned into weeks and months, and now it is the half-year mark. So today, I can say that it's half a year since my son died. I am surprised at how time flies and I also realise its power and cruel ruthlessness. Nobody can stand in its way.

Time is like a fast train running on its tracks at its own speed, not concerned with how many passengers cannot get off at their destination and how many people are left waiting at their stations. It does not change its route for anyone, neither does it turn back nor stop to wait for anybody.

O my Lord! Keep my child safe, exalt him and make his good deeds a permanent source of reward for him. Ameen.

He who used to live in my house
Has become a mere memory

Now he lives in his grave
He is no more than a memory

(Urfana Ayub)

7th July 2010

My friend called me today. Her mother had been ill for the last three to four weeks. She sounded quite worried and told me that her mother's condition has worsened. She had been moved to the hospital ICU. She asked me to pray for her.

At night I texted my friend to ask about her mother's condition, but she did not reply. Some time ago when Auntie was better, I went to visit her at her house. Then a few weeks ago, I went to the hospital to see her, but she was not fully conscious then and probably did not know about my visit.

When I woke up the next morning, a text message on my mobile told me about her death. My friend's mother passed away at 2:45 a.m that night.

The news disturbed me and my thoughts went to Adam. I went to my friend's house to console her and the whole episode of my son's departure and funeral flashed through my mind.

11. Our Family Pilgrimage

13th July 2010

Only two days are left before we proceed on our pilgrimage to the Holy Land. We all went to visit Adam in the graveyard and bade him goodbye. We were all upset to be leaving him. Ayub wept at Adam's grave. I handed him to God's protection.

Adam had wanted to be part of this family group to perform the pilgrimage (*Umrah*). Thanks to Allah almighty he performed his first pilgrimage with myself, his father, his paternal grand-father and with his younger brother, Ahmad. Allah (SWT) then gave him another opportunity to take part in Umrah, which he did with his paternal grandfather, Baba.

But it had long been our family wish that all of us; me, Ayub, all our children, their maternal uncles, together with their paternal aunt, uncles and Baba would perform the pilgrimage together. Adam always prayed with me for fulfilment of this wish, finishing with a loud "Ameen".

Whenever I prayed, "O God, I want to perform Umrah with my husband and all my children, please help me," I always felt apprehensive, like it was asking for too much and I was afraid that something would go wrong.

I had never thought that this trip would happen, or that it could be possible. But this was to be our year for our entire family to go together. So my main concerns were that everyone remained in good health, got holidays from our schools and colleges and leave from our workplaces, so that we could all travel in July.

It is a habit of mine that I ask my children to pray. I got this routine from my mother who used to make us supplicate when we were young, saying that God listens to children's prayers quickly. Whenever I made the children pray to God, Adam would always recite "Ameen" loudly in his heavy voice.

Today, Adam's voice saying "Ameen" was ringing in my ears. God had listened to his prayers. All of us were going except him. He was asleep in his last abode totally unaware of the world outside. But I know that if he had been here he would have been overjoyed at this itinerary. He would also have been very happy that his only and very beloved Phuphie was going with us too.

I prayed to Allah that, as Adam intended to perform the pilgrimage with the whole family, may Allah (SWT) reward him for his intentions even though he could not actually perform it, and have mercy on him (Ameen).

14th July 2010

Today's date has a special significance in my life. It is my twentieth wedding anniversary, thanks be to God. I got married at nineteen. Life after marriage was very different from the life I had lived during my first nineteen years. I left my country, my people, and what a coincidence that Adam left me when he was about nineteen! He even left this world. My son's departure introduced me to an entirely different world.

It revealed to me those signs of life and the hereafter of which

I had not been aware. Today, twenty years after my marriage, my life's first nineteen years and then nineteen years of my Adam's life have all passed. Now, in the twentieth year of marriage, I am standing at a new turn in life. A turn I thought I would never come to. It seems that the path I was travelling suddenly changed and this new direction came into view. My destination has also changed and the atmosphere around me is also evolving gradually. I am thankful to Allah for this transition in my life.

15th July 2010

We visited Adam's grave again before our departure. I bade him goodbye through tears. We were all ready to leave for Saudi Arabia.

Adam used to count on a black, beaded wooden rosary beads. I took that rosary (*Tasbeeh*) along with me. I also took Adam's framed photograph from Ammi's house, thinking that since Adam is not here, we will take his photo along and it will perform the pilgrimage. I planned to keep it with me throughout Umrah. I was convinced in my heart that God will accept the ritual on Adam's behalf.

He was not only present in the frame; he was living in my heart. O my Lord, please accept his presence and worship (Ameen).

16th July 2010
Makkah Mukarramah

Adam! Today we have safely reached Makkah Mukarramah. When my eyes fell on the Kaa'ba for the first time, I prayed for your forgiveness.

The scene which rejuvenates faith in the hearts of the Muslims is right in front of me. The Kaa'ba is a small stone building in the court of the Great Mosque that contains a sacred black stone. As it is the goal of all Islamic pilgrimage and the point to which Muslims all turn when praying, undoubtedly seeing the Kaa'ba for the first time is a very exalting experience. It evokes faith in the hearts of believers to see people of different colours, countries, nations and tribes congregated for the worship of one God. This time, the sight of the Kaa'ba invoked a different sensation in me. I saw God's power and my conviction in the "oneness" of God became absolute.

23rd July 2010
The Prophet's (Peace Be Upon Him) Mosque

Today I saw the mausoleum of The Holy Prophet Muhammad (Peace Be Upon Him). I prayed for everyone and kept thinking about you.

Last night I saw you in my dream. You were about fourteen or fifteen years of age. I was busy in the kitchen. You were getting ready to go somewhere. When I went to the room, you were gone. I kept calling you and crying after you. Suddenly, my dream was broken and I woke up. When I recollected the dream, I realised that you had actually gone from our lives.

Adam, a miracle happened today. Despite the crowd of people gathered around the mausoleum, I easily found a spot on the green carpet (*Riaz-ul-Jannah*)[1] to offer the necessary nafl prayer. This is a type of optional Muslim formal worship prayer. When I started offering the prayer for the second time,

1 *To show respect, Muslims are supposed to put PBUH or SAW Salallahu Alaihi Wa Salam, meaning Peace be upon him, after naming any and all prophets of Allah (SWT)*

93

I could not prostrate because of the multitude on all sides. Yet I felt as if a woman had flung both her arms around me. I quickly completed the prayer in the confines of her arms. That woman was no less than an angel for me. I felt as if Allah had sent invisible help for me. I thanked the woman and she embraced me. I kissed both her hands. Though we did not understand each other's language, we could perceive the feeling of gratitude between us.

I sat down to supplicate. The green dome of The Prophet's (Peace Be Upon Him) Mosque was before me, looking glamorous in the night lights. There I saw a middle-aged lady trying to push her wheel-chair. I went to her and asked her if she needed any assistance. She could not understand my language, so I enquired in sign language whether she wanted me to take her to the gate. She nodded her head in affirmation. Tears were rolling down my face as I pushed her wheelchair towards the gate, thinking that Allah had given me an opportunity to do a good deed. I do not deserve all the bounties that Allah (SWT) was showering on me, all praise be to Allah the almighty.

When we reached the gate, the lady in the wheelchair now experienced the same emotion as I had felt earlier. She kissed my hands, embraced me and prayed for me. My dear son, all these emotions are very beautiful.

I also visited Masjid-e-Quba² and Masjid-e-Qiblatain³ and offered nafl prayer at both these places on your behalf. During Isha prayer, the leader of the prayer (Imam) recited the following verse of the Holy Qur'an: "*Every living creature is bound to taste death*". *(Aal-I-ʿImran: 185, Holy Quran)*

2   The first Masjid built by the Holy Prophet *(PBUH)* near Madinah after his migration thereto.
3   The Masjid with two Qiblas (prayer direction). It was in this Masjid that during the prayer, Allah *(SWT)* commanded the Holy Prophet *(PBUH)* while he was leading the prayer, to change the prayer direction from Jerusalem to the Kaa'ba, which he did also all the followers in that prayer followed suit.

It seemed as if God was telling me that Adam has gone. Now I must also prepare to leave this world. This ayah was a reminder and a warning for me.

27th July 2010
The Prophet's *(Peace Be Upon Him)* Mosque

It is exactly seven months since you left us. I observed the fast for Shab-e-Baraa'at[4], praise be to God. My Lord gave me courage and forbearance. I am thinking of you again. Again, I remember when we used to sit together and prayed to perform the pilgrimage, you used to say "Ameen" in a loud voice, but for some reason, all this seems to be a memory of the remote past. I offered nafl prayers and supplication of du'as, for your forgiveness and prayed for you. This is the best gift I can send you now.

Arslan, Ambar and Ahmad went shopping. I thought if you were here, you would also have bought things for yourself. But this time, my shopping on your behalf consisted of prayers. I bought many rosary beads and distributed them amongst the women in the mosque to be a source of eternal reward for you. I also told them your name and asked them to specially pray for Mohammed Adam Ayub's forgiveness. In Sha Allah, soon you will receive all these prayers. May Allah (SWT) keep you in His protection.

We are going to Makkah Mukarramah tomorrow, where I plan to perform Umrah on your behalf. May Allah accept it Ameen.

---

4 *Meaning "Night of Exoneration", occurring on 15th o Shaa'ban, the 8th month of the Islamic calendar. Literally meaning "Madinah, the brightened one".*

28th July 2010

Adam, today we all have travelled to Makkah Mukarramah from Madinah Munawwarah[5] by coach. On our journey, we received the news that an Airblue airplane crashed on its flight from Karachi to Islamabad. The aircraft was destroyed and all 152 passengers were killed. This made me think of you again; that your sudden death brought grief to so many families. What would those one hundred and fifty seven passengers' families be going though after receiving the news of their loved ones' sudden death? Maybe now I can say that I do have an idea of their pain because I too have experienced it as a mother.

The same reality hits me, "What is life?" Somebody described it very well as a "bubble of water", meaning "very short and temporary"; like a little flame which is put out even by a mild wind. Most of the passengers on that plane would have considered it a short flight from Islamabad to Karachi. How could they have known that actually it was a long flight to their real and final destination?

I don't know whether those passengers bade farewell to their families. Usually in such circumstances, our reaction is, "It's only a matter of two hours. We will be back soon."

Adam, I was worried for those passengers. God knows whether they got a chance to recite the Kalima in the last moments of their life or not.

Sudden death is so heartbreaking and traumatic. May God protect everyone from it (Ameen). Though your departure was also very sudden, we easily managed to help you recite the Declaration of Faith and bade you farewell amongst prayers and love.

---

5   *Literally meaning "Madinah, the brightened one".*

30th July 2010
Makkah Mukarramah

Adam, I am very happy today. I got an opportunity to offer nafl prayers in the Hateem[6]. The previous two times when I was here, both on Hajj and on Umrah, I did not get a chance to offer nafl in the Hateem.

When your Phuphie and I were performing the circumambulation of the Kaa'ba, we decided to make an attempt to enter the Hateem. By God's Grace, we managed to go inside and both offered nawafil (plural of nafl) there.

Adam, if you had come here yourself, you would have performed just one pilgrimage for yourself, and now when you are not with us, we have all performed our second Umrahs on your behalf. Allah (SWT) willing, He will accept our worship and give its reward to you (Ameen).

31st July 2010
Makkah Mukarramah

Adam, a strange incident just happened to me. Maybe the incident itself was not as curious as I felt it to be. When we came out after circumambulation of the Kaa'ba , there was such a swarm of people that I could not see Ambar. I looked for her at our gate, but did not find her. Daddy was asleep. We went out to look for her again. We even tried to inform the police, but since we were not well-versed in Arabic, we could not make them understand.

We returned home terribly upset. In the meantime, one of the children woke Dad and told him that Ambar was missing. He,

6   The Hateem is the crescent-shaped area immediately adjacent to the Kaa'ba and an extremely rewarding place to perform nafl prayers.

too, went out to search for her. Everyone was shocked and extremely worried. I was engulfed with suspicions and premonitions. I felt your absence very acutely and was afraid that I would never see Ambar again either. I was frightened and wept a lot. Suddenly, Ambar arrived, smiling and eating ice cream. What a relief I felt! Ambar told me that she met her Phuphie and they both went to perform circumambulation of the Kaa'ba. Later, she bought ice cream and came home. She was totally oblivious of our concerns and fears.

Adam, ever since you went away, I dread that something terrible is going to happen, or that Allah will put me through some other test. I must always be ready. It is my humble and heartfelt fervent prayer to Allah that he may not put me through such circumstances that I cannot bear. May Allah give strength to my faith (*Iman*), Ameen.

1st August 2010
Makkah Mukarramah

Adam, I am sitting on the floor in front of the Kaa'ba's door and looking at the people performing circumambulation of the Kaa'ba. There is a separate section for women to worship here. It is 3:30 a.m. I have completed my prayer after the last prescribed prayer of the day.

I have brought your framed photograph with me. Adam, you are in the Kaa'ba and I am writing my diary. I want to spend time with you here in front of God's house so that I can pray for you.

When I took your photograph out of my bag, I felt moisture on the frame and back cover. I wondered how this could have happened. Then I remembered I had a small bottle of Zam

Zam in my bag. Holy Water must have leaked out of that bottle and seeped into the photograph frame. I thought of opening the frame and taking out the photograph to dry it, but due to moisture, the photograph was stuck to the frame.

I felt as if you have quenched your thirst with the Zam Zam. I closed the frame and put it back.

Then I met a lady who says, "Children are God's gift. They are like berries on a tree; some fall off the trees and others remain attached to them. Those which fall down are not ours, those which stay behind belong to us."

I am thankful to God that my tree still has three berries attached to it. You had to go, so you fell down. May your Creator's blessings be upon you, God willing.

Thank you, Adam

Thank you, Adam; your Phuphie is trying to fill in your absence here. I am always looking for you in her and she, too, is fulfilling all the obligations of a child.

I, being the only daughter of my parents, never knew a sister's love, and lately, I have begun to feel the absence of a sister. Now it seems as if God has fulfilled my desire. You know, Adam, I have always loved your aunt as a sister and a daughter, but still there was always a trifle of a distance between us. Now an unnamed shortfall in our relationship has been filled after your departure.

It seems as if I found my sister after you and a daughter who may one day take your place. Though your place is exclusively yours, and no one can actually take it, but if anyone comes close to it, it is your aunt. I can see you in her.

Now I can understand why Dadi Ammi could see Babur in you. These things only have to be understood and felt. If only we could understand the different relationships. Allah (SWT) created these relations for us to find solace and comfort in, but we create havoc with our relationships and family in this world. May Allah guide us to the right path and may He grant us the ability to stay connected with our blood relations. (Ameen)

Adam, yesterday, when I was going towards the Kaa'ba, I saw two young children wearing the pilgrimage white robes walking in front of me with their father. They seemed like you and Arslan in your old photographs. The elder of the two children had his arm around the younger one's shoulder like you always used to put your arm around Arslan's shoulders. I wished they would turn back and I would see that these two boys were my Adam and Arslan. Then I realised that it was only my imagination, a dream, a mother's heart's yearning. Tears welled in my eyes as I realised again that my Arslan's brother has gone away. His elder brother is no longer with him. The same brother who used to put his arm around his shoulders, who was not only his big brother, but was also his friend. No doubt, Arslan's brother Ahmad is with him, but he will always be younger than Arslan.

Adam, I am still sitting in the Kaa'ba mosque. It's 4:00 am in the morning. I feel as if, after writing my diary and talking to you, and after praying to Allah, that I have spent quality time with Allah (SWT) and with you. Having wept my heart out, I am feeling light now. May He always keep you safe (Ameen).

12. To Punjab & Family

3rd August 2010
Punjab, Pakistan

Adam, we have safely reached Pakistan after performing our pilgrimage. Your Phuphie, Uncle Abid and Uncle Yousaf have returned to England and we have come straight to Punjab. After meeting the relatives here, we will go to my mother's (Nani Ammi's) house in Karachi, and from there, back to England.

The grief of your separation has somehow renewed itself here. Everyone is talking about you. My aunts, uncles and cousins console me and talk to me about you.

Adam! I do not understand my own reactions sometimes. At times, I weep bitterly, and at other times I feel as if all my tears have dried up. I become depressed and withdrawn. I do not know how to respond to others or what to do. Everyone is sharing your memories and talking about you. Coming here and receiving so much love has really touched my heart. It has been quite a long time since my last visit to Punjab.

Some years back when I came to Punjab, the children of the relatives were very young. Now they are all grown up. I did not recognise many of them. Many people who were old then are no longer in this world now.

Nature's cycle is very enigmatic. I met my Auntie Naseem's children after her death and again felt the same thing which amazes me. When somebody dies, nothing stops. Everything continues as before, sometimes maybe better than before, because God is the One who keeps the universe revolving. It is a mistake to think of ourselves as indispensable.

When Khala (Aunty) was alive, she dreamed about getting her youngest children, twin boys, married. But God had not ordained it so. This did not stop nature's cycle. Both sons got married by God's will after her death.

Adam, I am exhausted. Ever since I left our home in England, I have been in a state of constant journey. My heart is depressed. In a few days, I will go to Karachi to meet my parents.

10th August 2010
Karachi

When I met my parents and your uncles (*Mamoons*) at the airport, everyone was sad. Meeting me did not abate their sorrow, because this time I had gone to meet them without you.

They were all anxiously waiting for us to arrive from our pilgrimage. When my mother, Nani Ammi, saw me without my Adam, she could not hold back her tears. Although I had met my family very bravely, she cried throughout the journey home.

Everyone here remembered you and talked about you daily. Everyone prayed for you too, All praise is due to God. Adam, here too you have found so much love from all your maternal relatives. You are the firstborn of their only daughter. Your personality was so pleasant that everyone loved and adored you.

Your father and the children still have a few extra days of holidays left, so they will stay here for some more time. But I am returning to England on 14th August.

14th August 2010
Karachi Airport

Adam, I have reached the airport departure lounge after bidding farewell to everyone. Sometimes it seems a little strange that I am going alone, but on the other hand, I feel as if you are waiting for me so I will not be on my own once I reach England.

Since your grave is in Bradford, it seemed you were not in Pakistan. So I will come to meet you in Bradford. Adam, I will reach home late tonight. But tomorrow, God willing, I will definitely come to see you.

Just now when I was writing the diary, a lady whose family had been waiting nearby for some time asked if I was a writer or a novelist. Tears came to my eyes. I told her what I was writing and why. Adam, I am a little surprised at the lady's enquiry. Maybe I was so much absorbed in my own world that I was unaware of my surroundings. That is why she asked me. On hearing my answer, she too became sad and consoled me.

My dear Adam, I am neither a writer nor a poetess. Separation from you has taught me to write. Sometimes I am at a complete loss, unsure what to write or feel. I am sitting in the plane right now but I do not feel alone at all. It seems you are travelling with me.

When Arslan, Ambar and Ahmad are with me, I can see their

faces and touch them. The difference with you is that you are living in my mind and heart. I can neither touch you nor see you.

Everything seems trivial after you. Meeting people, going to places and everything else makes me realise the truth of this untrustworthy world. Every day, every gesture, every sentiment makes me aware of the fact that being separated from you has taught me many lessons. May Allah reward you with goodness, son.

13. Home to Bradford

19th August 2010

Ever since I have returned to England, you are constantly in my thoughts. It is partly due to the fact that Dad and the other children are still in Pakistan. It seems odd that, though you are here with me in Bradford, you are still not in our house. You are in your final earthly abode, your grave. Two days back I kept thinking of you and crying the whole day. I kept thinking of the things you used to say, as I went through your belongings.

Today, I visited your grave again. It was raining lightly. The graveyard was empty and I could not help thinking that the houses outside the graveyard have so many comforts like curtains, sofas, carpets, heating, etc. People are trying to reach their destinations quickly and take shelter because of the rain outside. They do not want to get wet. But you are in your grave.

Those who are dead remain in their graves irrespective of what the conditions are outside - rain, sun, storm, cold, dark or snow. They are not afraid of anything.

All such concerns are for the people of this world. Our indifference is also for this world only. Why have we become so callous?

Oh, Adam! No man nor university could have taught me the reality of life and its transience the way you did. May Allah reward you with goodness, my son!

22nd August 2010

This morning I went to the graveyard to meet you. In reality, I do not go there only to meet you; I also go there to remind my own self that I too have to come here one day. This is my destination as well. Doing this enhances my faith.

As somebody very aptly said:

> *O traveller of the world, your destination is the grave*
> *What you travel through here (life) is very temporary*
> *Since the world came into existence, millions of people have been born*
> *None of them lived forever; all were buried in their graves never forget, this is every man's destiny*
> *O traveller of the world, your destination is the grave*
> *How many funerals have you seen with your eyes?*
> *How many people have your hands buried?*
> *Why are you so oblivious to your own end?*
> *O traveller of the world, your destination is the grave*
> *Those who used to sleep in their velvet beds are now sleeping in the earth*
> *The kings and beggars are all sleeping in the earth together*
> *Death has made them all equal*
> *O traveller of this world, your destination is the grave*
> *This luxurious house of yours is useless now*
> *These tall buildings are useless*
> *Your home is now just two yards of earth*
> *O traveller of the world, your destination is the grave*
> *You came into the world one day and one day you will leave it*
> *O traveller of this world, your destination is the grave*
> *What you travel through in this world (life) is very short*

Uncle Yousaf and Aunt Arshia invited me to their place for a meal to end my fast today and insisted that I stay the night with them. This is our old house where you spent your childhood. Now Yousaf lives there with his family.

Their house somehow seemed different this time. I have so many memories associated with it. Memories of this house and memories of your childhood. Adam, I could see you sitting and playing in every room. All those scenes from the past were flashing through my mind.

You were about four years old when we bought this house and moved here from your grandmother's house. Do you remember Ambar was very young then? You spent about eleven years of your life in this house, from five years of age to sixteen. Every corner of this house is filled with your memories.

I went to offer prayer in the front room. There, my eyes fell on the showpiece in the cabinet which Uncle Babur (*Chachcha*) had sent. It bore your name. Seeing your name brought tears to my eyes.

> *This name is now your memory*
> *Talking about you is your memory*
> (Urfana Ayub)

When I see the name "Adam" written anywhere, I feel as if it is related to me only. Actually, many Adams come into this world and then pass away. This is Nature's system. I will stay the night in the same room which used to be yours, but not finding you there puzzles me. Everybody else is here; your things and your room are here, too, but you are not.

Why is a human being's existence such that after his death,

it seems as though he never came into this world? But your memories tell me that you did come into this world. Your belongings tell me that yes, you did come.

Nothing stops when someone dies. Everything keeps going like before. May Allah (SWT) grant you a place in the highest heaven. (Ameen)

27th August 2010

Adam! It is exactly eight months today since you went away. We all went to the graveyard. Arslan and Ahmad cleaned your grave. Your smiling face never fades away from my memory or my eyes. I see your face regardless of whether my eyes are open or closed. Now I have reached the stage when even during the daily prayers (*Namaaz*), your face fills my eyes and mind. I prayed to God and asked for His forgiveness.

"Oh Allah! I worship only You. Please remove the thoughts of my son from my mind. I do not want to disobey you ever."

How did I spend these eight months? Could someone ask me...?

On the other hand, these eight months have passed so quickly that I fail to understand. Four months from now it will be one full year since your departure. Very soon, these months will convert into years. The 27th of every month will always remind me of you leaving us.

When I see you in this mound of mud, I realise that only this is real. All of us will be buried in the earth one day and will become mud, too. Only our spirit and good deeds will be left.

For me, the reality of life is your grave
The story starts and again finishes here
(Urfana Ayub)

When one is alive, even a small stain on our clothes or a bad odour from them makes us change the clothes immediately. We are so particular about these things. You were also very fond of wearing nice and clean clothes. Everyone thought of you as a very well-dressed individual. Today, stray weeds are growing on your grave. Insects and moths are crawling nearby. It's not only your grave; all the other ones are in a similar shape. On some graves, the weeds have grown into full trees and some are in such a dilapidated condition that one feels sorry for them.

But you are asleep in your grave, totally oblivious of what is happening outside it. The truth is that our deeds, whether good or bad, will accompany us in the grave. If they are good, they will light up the grave. I pray, my son, that your grave be illuminated, fragrant and spacious and may God grant you an abode in the highest heaven. Ameen.

14. Ramadhan Without You

5th September 2010

I participated in a Khatam-ul-Qur'an (completion of Qur'an) ceremony in Leeds today. You were spoken about in that ceremony.

Tonight is the 27th night of Ramadhan. I remembered last year's 27th Ramadhan when we all went to the mosque for worship and prayers (*Ibaadah*). Tonight, we will again go to listen to Qur'an but you will not be with us.

At first, my association with the city of Leeds was because of you. You used to go there to the City Hospital for your regular check-ups, but some time before your departure, I developed a new association with Leeds through attending Qur'an classes. When I went to the city for the first time after your death, a strange sensation came over me, but as the signs for Leeds General Infirmary came into view, instead of turning towards the hospital, I went towards the Qur'an class. I realised that my link with Leeds was not only through the hospital or your death. I have formed another very strong bond with this city, and that is through my weekly Qur'an classes. I should come here happily, not with sorrow.

Now I enjoy a beautiful relationship with Leeds City, All praise is due to God.

6th September 2010
27th Night of Ramadhan

We all went to the Masjid for worship (*Ibaadah*). There I encountered the lady whom I had met last year whose son had died from his heart condition. She had asked about Adam then and I had thanked God that my son was alive.

Today, neither her son nor mine are alive. My situation was similar to that of the other mother. This is God's will. Adam, your absence from this world puts me in a strange frame of mind and this feeling brings me closer to God. My own existence seems very trivial and insignificant.

Now I am more aware of the breaking down going on inside me. The outside world is also not the same for me anymore, but the greatest change is in my feelings and perception. Nothing is like before. I am much more sensitive and aware of the hereafter and am always in a process of getting ready to go somewhere. I do not want to get involved in this world and this rekindles my hope of meeting you. All praise is due to God.

10th September 2010
Eid-ul-Fitr

Our first Eid without you and everyone has been thinking of you since morning. Your absence was distressing for everybody. My eyes were seeking you and my ears were longing to hear your voice.

I asked the family to dress up appropriately for Eid. It is not a day to grieve. All praise is due to Allah (SWT) for it is a day to rejoice and to thank Allah that we were blessed to have had

Adam enter our lives, even for a short time.

You were like a fragrance who perfumed the whole environment and then went away. You gave us wonderful memories before leaving us. You were God's beautiful creation. You were a source of blessing for the whole family because you taught us the value of relationships.

Your departure mended many family ties which were broken; there are only a few people who can boast of such ability. Allah (SWT) had graced you with a special talent to spread good deeds. I fervently pray to Allah (SWT) that all the good deeds which have taken place because of your death may become a source of permanent reward for you. Ameen.

Love you, Adam.

In the words of an unknown poet:

> *Whenever we see the Eid's moon*
> *Oh departed one, we long for you*

I did not have any idea how I would be feeling today. I thought that, as a few months have passed since your departure, I would be strong now. Alas no! Tears kept rolling the whole day incessantly. Your memory is like a shadow which I desperately try to hold on to, but I fail every time and this tires me.

I must realise that you are, in fact, a shadow, and that I can never have you like I did when you lived in our house. The health and strength which Allah has blessed me with must be used positively and constructively to carry out noble deeds. I am also acutely aware of the fact that Allah (SWT) has graced us with countless bounties and fortunes, but how ungrateful we are. If Allah chooses to take back even one out of those countless bounties, we start complaining, whining and grieving over it.

O Allah! Make us one of your chosen people who acknowledge your bounties and protect us from the afflictions of the devil. (Ameen)

I was listening to Ahmed Bukhtiar's nasheed, "*Forgive Me*", in which he says,

> *If I have two legs, then the whole world is mine,*
> *If I can hear, the whole world is mine.*

We do not thank Allah (SWT) for the healthy organs He has blessed us with. We must be grateful for our hands, feet, sight, and hearing and for so countless other blessings that we usually take for granted.

We see many people around us who are deprived of these blessings, but we do not learn from them; neither do we prostrate before Allah (SWT) in gratitude. May Allah (SWT) guide us to the path of gratefulness and forgiveness (Ameen).

16th September 2010

I went to the hospital to see Uncle Abid. He had surgery on his leg. There was a lot of traffic on the road. Then I noticed that the car in front of me bore a number plate with your name on it.

My mind flashed back to when you used to say, "When I learn to drive, we will go to buy a car together." You used to point out cars on the road saying, "We will buy this sort of a car, Okay?" I never thought that you would leave us before your driving test and we would never be able to buy a car together.

113

Now Arslan says the same thing. "When I pass my driving test we will buy a car. Okay, Mum?"
And I always reply, "God willing (In Sha Allah)."

A few days back I saw a van parked outside with the words "Adams Construction" written boldly on it. Whenever I see your name, I go into a trance for some time. Then the realisation comes that Adam was not only my son. Many other people are also called Adam. My Adam is not in this world anymore.

15. Trying To Keep Busy

27th September 2010

Today, it is exactly nine months since you went away. My feelings are somewhat different today. It is not a matter of another month passing by, but of the time period which you spent with me outside this world. The nine months which you spent in my womb, then about nineteen years in this world and now it is nine months since you left us.

Nine months before your birth - your lifespan - nine months after your death.

Today this stage is also completed. After three months it will be one full year and after that the years will keep accumulating. I am amazed at the speed of time. The passing time sometimes fades out and at other times seems clearer than ever. Why do memories become history?

The glamour and attraction of life has dwindled considerably for me after your departure. Maybe it is because I have learnt the truth about it. Now the worth of a diamond ring does not seem more than that of an ordinary stone ring. Large beautiful mansion-like houses seem no more than brick walls. Everything seems worthless. The reality is only what you showed me.

Adam! I try not to think of you often so I keep myself busy. But it is easier said than done.

There is never a moment, a day, a morning or an evening

when I do not think of you. But still I keep trying to put your memories aside and move on in life.

I do not want your thoughts to tie me down and prevent me from moving ahead and fulfilling the task God has ascribed to me. That is why I neither watch your family videos nor sit alone with your photo albums. I simply keep praying and supplicating for you the whole day throughout my daily duties.

I also keep explaining to myself that I have fulfilled my duty towards you. Allah (SWT) has released you. Your father and I are free of all our obligations towards you. You have gone away from us, and I know that wherever you are, you are very happy and content, but I cannot go there to meet you yet. All praise is due to Allah (SWT) Adam, your departure has given me the insight that I, too, should start preparing for my departure. May Allah (SWT) reward you for this noble deed of yours. Ameen.

Adam, today I am wearing your thick, brown jumper. You know I cannot tolerate cold. Dear son, may you be in God's protection. God protect you.

13th October 2010

Adam! Today I attended a marriage ceremony for the first time after you left us. It was the wedding of my friend's daughter who is about your age. My friend and I both are of the opinion that children should be married young. When she came to give me the invitation card, my mind filled with your thoughts. I often used to talk about marriage with you. It was my desire to get you married immediately after you completed your studies so I could become a grandmother.

I did not know myself how I would feel as I watched this wedding ceremony. When the bride and groom were being escorted towards the stage amidst the beating of a dhoal[1], I could not hold back my tears. I was thinking of your departure. The thought of your funeral and the crowd of people came to my mind. Many times I have tried to hold back this ocean and have tried to console myself. I am ever thankful to Allah (SWT) that you reached your eternal abode with respect and grace, All praise is due to Allah (SWT).

This morning I met a woman who had only one son, a single boy amongst five sisters, who died in an accident at twelve years of age. I think of that mother who has no son left, and I thank Allah (SWT) that if He has taken one son from me, He has blessed me with two more sons.

Adam! I could not go to the graveyard today. It rained the whole day and I was a little busy, too. I knew you would not be angry with me, nor would you complain. Adam, I am deeply sad and missing you. Please come in my dream and talk to me. I am mentioning this for the first time in my diary. I will be waiting for you. God protect you.

17th October 2010

Adam, I attended another wedding today. I picked up a lot of courage to be at this ceremony. When I heard the bride and groom being brought to the stage and wedding songs playing in the background, my heart yearned dearly for you. All that I used to say to you regarding your wedding flashed through my mind. If you were here, I would have got you married in two to three years' time.

---

1 *A drum beaten with sticks on both sides, traditionally from the Punjab region of Pakistan and India*

117

I am also grateful for the fact that, last year when you expressed your wish to wear a Sherwani, I fulfilled your desire and bought one for you. Allah (SWT) intended me to see you clad in a Sherwani. Your wish to wear a Sherwani was also put in your heart by Allah (SWT) because He knew of His intention to summon you back.

I remember being a bit surprised at your request at that time, because under ordinary circumstances, you would not have expressed such a wish. This was only Allah (SWT)'s doing; that I may see you wearing the robe which is associated primarily with bridegrooms only, because Allah (SWT) knew I would never witness your wedding day. This was all Allah (SWT)'s Wisdom, All praise is due to Allah (SWT). Yet I felt that it was difficult for me to attend this marriage ceremony.

Weddings always seem to remind me of your departure. The arrival of your coffin, the gathering of people, having the meal, your going away. It was all part of your farewell. While I was eating at the wedding, my eyes filled with tears and I could not even see the food clearly. At the same time, I was evading people's looks so that they could not know my emotions. I kept sitting with eyes downcast.

An unknown poet sums up my feelings:

I don't know which tear of mine would tell my story to a stranger
That is why I am sitting with my eyes lowered.

I prayed for the wedding couple that Allah (SWT) may keep them happy, Ameen. It is also my heartfelt prayer that Allah (SWT) may protect my son and keep him happy and content, Ameen.

26th October 2010

Amsterdam

The children had holidays from their schools for a few days so we have all come to the Netherlands for a short break. We roamed about the whole day and now we have finally come back to rest after a very tiring excursion. The difference with this vacation is that your Phuphie is with us instead of you. My heart was lonely and desolate. I was missing you very intensely. I remember last year when we tried to go on a holiday, we missed the ferry and lost the chance of having a family vacation. Like last year, we bought pizzas on the way.

Your framed photograph goes with me everywhere. You are here with me in Amsterdam too.

You know that your Nana Abbu is not well these days. He was running a high-grade fever for which he was admitted to hospital. I am worried for him. May Allah grant him health (Ameen). Adam, the relationship between parents and children is very unique. One can find a replacement for anything else in this world except for these relationships. If they are lost, we will never find their like anywhere else.

Adam, your Dadi loves you very much. Her eyes fill with tears at the mere mention of your name. She misses you terribly. I never knew that she adored you so much. She cries a lot for you. Even when I go to her house with composure and strength, she talks of you and makes me cry.

A few verses from your Dadi to you:

> *I have loved you with the core of my spirit*
> *I am alive, confined to the solitude of my being*

I entrust you to the protection of Allah (SWT), my son. May He be your guardian, Ameen!

27th October 2010

Ten months have passed since you went away. Who can hold back the time? It is not passing; it is running. I get scared of the speed of time.

I become apprehensive too that I will also be summoned back to God suddenly like you. But I am not afraid of dying anymore. I am only worried that I have not prepared adequately for it. I have not packed even a handbag or a suitcase. How will I face my Creator?

I fervently pray to Allah (SWT) that He may give me some time to make preparations so that I may be successful in the Hereafter (Ameen).

After a long while Adam, I saw you in my dream. You came home with your Dadi Ammi. I was very happy to see you, but even during the dream I was aware of the fact that you have gone away from this world. I had not even spoken to you when my dream ended. When I woke up, you were nowhere. Whenever I see you in my dream, I desperately want to hug you and talk to you.

7th November 2010

Adam, today I attended another wedding ceremony. Now these weddings make me sad. Tears fall uncontrollably and I became acutely conscious of the fact that I will never be able to see you dressed up like a groom. I will not become a grandmother of your children. Do you remember how Ahmad used to tease you about girls? He said he would dance at your wedding and create a lot of commotion and merry-making.

The Sherwani which you wore last Eid is hanging in my wardrobe. When I look at it, I travel back in time and see you wearing it. In the wedding ceremony, I met a lady who got her nineteen- year-old son married a few months ago. She introduced her daughter-in-law to me. I gave a dua for the couple, but my own heart became depressed.

Adam, you are not aware of the gift which you have given me! You have taught me the correct way of living this life!

I was alone in the hustle and bustle of the wedding ceremony, trying to hide my tears. My inner self was sad and desolate. This loneliness was within me. The outside world was full of excitement, the beautiful environment, shimmering dresses, exquisite jewellery, pretty people and different types of elaborate food. But I felt that these extravaganzas move us away from God. When a heart beats without God's name (*zikr* - remembrance of Allah) it becomes more vacant, more desolate. Adam, I am trying to liven up my heart with God's remembrance and His love.

When you went away, everybody around me supported me, helped me to bear the loss, and sympathised with me, but my real Sustainer is Allah. He gave me courage, guided me, helped me to overcome my grief and granted patience to me. What a blessing patience is! No doubt there is no blessing like patience.

I wept and supplicated to my Lord and in return He granted me an abundance of patience, All praise is due to Allah (SWT). Your death challenged my faith. It was a huge challenge! I am trying to remain steadfast in this test. Framed prayers for the forgiveness of the deceased are hung in every room of the house. These will keep reminding me of you. You are living in everyone's memories. May Allah (SWT) be your guardian, Ameen. Adam, for some days, a thought has been striking me repeatedly. I want to publish this diary of mine in a book form. I want to share my grief and emotions with everyone. I do not take this grief as a gloom. It has shown me the way to live a new life.

But if it is sorrow, it is a very welcome and gratifying sorrow. In fact, it is such a beautiful sorrow that I want other people to experience it as well. I hope that this diary, which has become a source of solace for me, may provide relief to other people, too.

When I started writing this diary, my sole purpose was to transfer my feelings onto paper. You know, Adam, I have never written a diary before. Neither have I written any poem. I was only fond of reading good poetry, but I had no desire for writing. However, when I started writing this diary, it seemed I had found a companion to whom I could tell anything. I felt light after writing. A few months later, my style of writing changed and I automatically started addressing you. This made me feel more content. I could feel you around me and I felt as if I was narrating my deepest feelings to you.

I know that you have left this world and gone to your Creator. You cannot hear me, but this unique feeling that I can talk to you, tell you things, take your advice and address you is very gratifying.

The one and only purpose of publishing this book is to spread my message. This message is for all those people who have lost a dear one: either a mother losing her son, like me, or an Ambar losing her brother Adam. Or maybe, it is a boy who has lost his elder brother, like my Arslan and Ahmad did. Or it is a father mourning his son, like Ayub, or maybe a person who lost a dear friend or grandparents who missed their grandson or granddaughter, or a husband or wife who must go on without their spouse. There is a long list of such loved ones. At times, these relationships and friendships do not even have a name but their departure leaves a vacuum behind.

An unknown poet expresses it best:

> *He has gone to his abode, do not mourn him*
> *That much was his, stay here, do not mourn him.*

Do not grieve for those who have gone away. I know it is easier said than done. Only he can understand whose body is hurt.

My father always remarked, "I do not understand why people use the word "grief" when someone dies. Grief for what? One should be happy that he has reached his Creator safely."

I could never comprehend the meaning of it, but now I can! It is all a matter of insight. If one understands it, life becomes easy. If not, it becomes a burden.

Adam, as I was telling you, I am thinking of publishing this diary. Please pray to Allah (SWT) that He may help me succeed in this endeavour, Ameen.

16. Snow Season Comes Again

15th November 2010
Eid ul Adha

> *My eyes are moist in the memory of departed ones (souls)*
> *How can I decorate my house this Eid morning?*

> *(Unknown poet)*

Adam, this is our first Eid-ul-Adha without you. I am missing you very much since yesterday. My eyes are looking for you. I made your favourite dessert, ras malai (a traditional sweet made from condensed milk). After the Eid-ul-Adha, when we all assembled for family worship, I thought of last year's Eid when you were also sitting with us.

I don't know what came over me back then when I asked you to recite supplication. Otherwise, every year it was daddy who recited it. I remember I was very pleased with your dua. It was a very detailed prayer in which you mentioned everybody's name. When I asked you whether you always prayed like this for everyone, you replied, "Mum, I recite this whole supplication after each prayer." I felt very pleased and content at your answer.

It was also God's blessing that He gave you a chance to do a collective prayer for everyone on your last Eid with us.

Like every year, we spent the rest of the day at Ammi's house. Adam, now I cannot give you anything on Eid except supplication, although there is no better gift for you now.

As a poet said:

With tears in my eyes, shining like lamps
I have come to give you the Eid gift.

Do you remember, Adam, whenever I gave Eidi (money given by elders to the children on the occasion of Eid) to you, you distributed it amongst the other children? This year I told Arslan to give Eidi to the other kids because he is the eldest brother now. This way children will not feel Adam's absence.

27th November 2010

Adam, it is the 27th of the month once again and incidentally the same day of the week, a Sunday. The whole of yesterday I kept remembering and thinking of you. Tears flowed unceasingly. I was painfully aware of the fact that eleven months have passed.

When I got up this Sunday morning, everything was covered with snow, which again is a sign of your memory and departure from this world. Last year, the snowfall was the heaviest in many years and you left us in that same snow season.

How I remember your smile. All the time I am looking for excuses to forget you. But no matter how busy I keep myself, your memory does not leave me even for a moment. I do not want to part from these memories either. They are a precious asset of mine.

Today a letter arrived for Ahmad. He had participated in a poetry competition and his poem was selected to be published in a book. We were so pleased at the news. Parents cherish even the smallest success of their children.

I remember when you got your letter of admission to university, a strange feeling of elation came over me. Maybe it was because my eldest child had reached college level. I realised then that although many people attend college and it is nothing extraordinary. But my emotion and happiness were unique.

And when you entered university, I felt like such a proud parent. By the grace of God, my son was old enough to go to university. Another event which made me happy and proud was when you started learning to drive.

The heart is so naive. It fills with joy like a small child and is offended easily, too. These emotions and sentiments make up our lives. Life is a mix of joys and sorrows.

Adam, the uncle (elderly man) who lived next to your Dadi Ammi's house died today. We received the news in the morning that the funeral prayer (*Namaz-e-Janaza*) will be held after the midday prayer in the same mosque where your funeral prayer was offered.

When we reached the Masjid, the coffin was placed in the ladies' section exactly in the same location where yours had been. The day was also Sunday, at the same time of day and the same season, too. Somebody's father, husband, brother and son departed from this world today.

Today's day and date were a matter of coincidence, but everyone's departure is exactly according to the schedule set by Allah (SWT). Attending this funeral brought memories of your departure back.

1st December 2010

Adam, do you know what happened yesterday? I was feeling very low and depressed so I went to bed early. I woke up at 11 p.m. Some words came to my mind which reflected my most heartfelt feelings. So I wrote them down. This morning, when I read those words, I realised it was a complete poem. I was surprised at myself. I, who had never even written a couplet, could compose a whole poem! Adam, I wish you could read it.

The title of the poem is;
I Don't Know Where He Is Lost

I don't know where he is lost
The one whom I loved so dearly, where is he lost?
He was part of my being, how could this happen?
The agony I am passing through
I had never thought would afflict me
The one who was part of my life is now only a dream
I don't know where he is lost,
I don't know how this happened
Even today my heart sinks when I think of him
Was he real or just a story?
Whoever he was, he was very dear to me
He was part of my being,
I don't know where he is lost
His coming in this world was Allah's blessing
His departure is Allah's Wisdom
He strengthened many ties
He broke many relations
He was loved by all
I don't know where he is lost,
I don't know how this happened
I am amazed at myself,
I, who was unfamiliar with words

How could I compose a poem?
How come this has been written?
My heart is sorrowful, my eyes filled with tears
But a ray of hope is lighting the way
Adam! Your mother's prayers are with you always
May Allah (SWT) grant you the highest place in Jannah
Where are you lost?
How did this happen?
I have accepted my destiny
I ask Allah (SWT) just for patience What happened so suddenly?
I don't know where you are lost,
I don't know how this happened.

(Urfana Ayub)

17. I Am Taken Ill

5th December 2010

I was not well today and had to go to hospital. When my blood was drawn for tests, I thought of you. I remember you were terrified of needles. Like myself, you too never liked blood tests. I used to encourage you and tried to dissipate your anxieties. Though I used to put on a brave show, in reality, I was more scared than you.

I was thinking of last December when you went to hospital and then left us forever. Adam, there are so many things which I will never be able to talk to you about. I am trying very hard to find your replacement in Arslan and I know he is also trying his level best that your father and I should not feel your absence.

For instance, something happened a few days ago which I wanted to talk over with you. If you had heard it you would have smiled too. Anyway, I told Arslan about it. As I said, I am trying my best to accept the fact that now Arslan is my eldest son.

Whenever someone asks me regarding my children, I still reply, "I have four kids."

Adam, you were the first one to confer motherhood on me, but now the fact is that you are gone, gone forever. I cannot evade the truth and live under false hopes. I fully accept God's will.

Adam, your brothers and sister are stronger than your parents. We all talk about you in the house. Occasionally, Ambar breaks down in front of me, though she tries not to show it, so that nobody should see her upset. Arslan has kept himself very composed. In other words, he does not share his grief with anyone.

Sometimes I get worried for Arslan. I want him to cry and let off steam. His brother and friend have left this world. Do you remember he used to fight with you over petty things? May Allah (SWT) grant him health, strength and perseverance (Ameen). I cannot comprehend the intensity of his grief for it is too much. He had only one elder brother, All praise is due to Allah (SWT). I have two more sons.

6th December 2010

Adam, I got admitted to hospital today. I remember you were often admitted to hospital. You used to come here for your check-ups, but you liked neither the hospital nor the check-ups.

All praise is due to Allah (SWT) for I have never had an illness in my life besides influenza and mild fever. Neither have I stayed in hospital. This was my first experience to spend the night there. The nurses visited me repeatedly to check my blood pressure, take my temperature and draw blood for various tests.

This whole experience made me relive the time last year when you came to hospital for your check-up. I met many people during my stay. Every person has his own story. The lady on the bed next to mine was just told by the doctor that she has cancer. She was very surprised by the news as I would have been if the doctor had, God forbid, given me such a diagnosis. No one in life is prepared for such news or thinks that he/she will suffer from cancer. This makes me realise how a person's life can change in a single moment.

I sympathised with that lady. She will undergo emergency surgery today. I am waiting for test results too. I realised that the result could be anything from good to bad. I am not thinking this because I am a pessimistic person, but because things can happen in an instant, like when you went away so suddenly or this lady got news of her cancer. Anything can happen to anybody.

I asked myself,

"Am I prepared to go?"
"What will happen to my children?" "What will happen to my husband?"

But I was content with the answer I got. I am not at all afraid of death. I was not even worried for my husband and children, and neither did it occur to me how and who will run my house if I die. Do you know, Adam, Allah (SWT) has given me this strength and taught this to me because of you?

"Man comes alone in this world and will go from here alone". The relationships and connections of this world seem dear to us whilst we are alive. But when death approaches, every-one will be concerned about themselves only. On the Day of Judgment, if a person requires just one good deed for salvation, no mother will be prepared to give it to her son and no husband will be prepared to give it to his wife. Adam, I had only one concern when I asked myself whether I was prepared to meet my Creator, which was that I have not prepared myself adequately. I have neither a suitcase nor a handbag of good deeds prepared. The realisation came very forcefully that I need a lot of preparation. There are so many things I want to do from a religious point of view.

I want to take religious education classes, I want to understand the Qur'an, I want to learn the Arabic language. Basically, I want to serve my religion and I need time to fulfil my wishes. I pray to God to give me sufficient life and health to achieve all this. If I manage to live my life in this manner I might be able to please God (Ameen).

I met another lady who was to undergo emergency surgery. She was concerned about her one-year-old daughter whom she had left with her husband. She told me that Allah (SWT) had blessed her with a daughter fifteen years after marriage. She had left her daughter alone for the first time and was worried how the little girl would spend the night without her mother. A woman came over to me and asked me about you, Adam, and expressed her sympathy. She was an acquaintance of your Dadi Ammi who recognised me, but I did not know her. She asked me about my other children. In response, I, too, asked her about her children. She told me very sadly that she did not have any. I thought that surely a couple would be blessed with children after fifteen years of marriage, but this is not always so. Some people are not blessed with children at all and some people are, but later, Allah (SWT) takes them away.

Our Lord blesses whoever He wishes with whatever He wishes. We do not understand His distribution of bounties. Adam, my uncle Khalid (my Mamoon) once recited a Punjabi poem to me by an unknown poet, which I liked very much:

My Lord has blessed those who ask Him each one with different bounties
Nobody can understand the distribution of His graces

To whom He will give a million and to whom He will give
nothing My heart was full of love
He gave me more than I expected I only want to prostrate
before Him
I do not care where I bow

A similar scenario happened with me, All praise is due to God.

8th December 2010

Adam, I have come home from the hospital. My mother called from Pakistan in the morning. She sounded very worried. In fact, she was crying. She had not eaten properly for three days because she was so concerned for my health. She did know that I was ill, but was worried because she did not know how poorly I was. However, she was relieved after talking to me and learning that it was just a minor temporary illness and that I am going to recover completely, All praise is due to Allah (SWT).

She said, "I think of Adam all the time. He was my first grandson, the first son of my only daughter. Though he was very dear to all of us, I cannot comprehend the intensity of your grief since you are his mother." If I was unwell here for the last three days; in Pakistan she was so worried for me that she fell ill herself and had to go to hospital.

She was trying to encourage me so that I could be strong. I thought if my mother worried herself to the stage of becoming sick because of my illness, what would be the condition of a mother who loses her child?

That is why she said, "I cannot pretend to understand your

sorrow because it is far too big, but you are a very strong woman. I became ill because my daughter was sick. If something bad happens to her, what will I do?"

I kept listening to her in silence and crying at the same time. How unique these relationships are! How much affection there is between them! There is no substitute, especially the relationship between parents and children. No one can get a child in lieu of something and neither can anybody be a replacement for parents.

Adam, do you know the Islamic month of Muharram has begun? A happy New Islamic Year to us all. May God keep guard over you and give you the best of everything (Ameen). In a few days, it will be exactly a full year since your departure. May God bless you my child and give you the highest rewards in the highest heaven (Ameen).

Whenever I write, I see the reflection of your smiling face in the paper. May Allah (SWT) keep you happy always in your eternal life (Ameen).

18. A New Year

Adam, today when I went to drop off Arslan at school, I passed that plum tree which had bowed under the weight of its fruit during summer. I remember when I first saw it, I was quite surprised at the amount of fruit present on even a single branch. Maybe I had never seen this much fruit on one tree before, or else I had never noticed.

Now that tree was completely bare and dried up. Not even one of its branches was green. There was not even a hint of life. Its branches bore neither leaves nor fruit. While looking at the tree I started meditating on God's power and might and comparing the tree with the essence of human life. It reflects both life and death.

God reveals clear signs of His strength to us. If only we could understand! Every year during autumn season, the trees become bare and unappealing. Their leaves become yellow and fall off. It seems as if there was never any life in them. Then by God's grace, the same trees bear leaves and buds in spring. They become loaded with flowers and fruit. This reflects the end of human life and the beginning of eternal life after death.

10th December 2010

During the Friday sermon, the Imam highlighted the importance of the Islamic month of Muharram. He pointed out that many people who were amongst us last Muharram are dead now and no one knows how many of us will not be with us this time next year.

I felt as if he was talking about you, Adam. Do you remember at the beginning of last Muharram, you sent a text message to everyone which conveyed a similar meaning? Yesterday when I went to your Dadi Ammi's house, we talked about your passing away. It seems strange that in one year, the date of your departure is falling on two different days. This year, 10th Muharram will be on December 16th, whereas last year it was on the 27th (the Islamic calendar (which is based on the movement of the moon) is slightly shorter than the Gregorian calendar (which based of the movement of the sun) by usually 10 days). I will think of you and miss you on both these days. It is also Allah's special favour that we will remember you on this prestigious Islamic day and devote ourselves to prayers at the same time, not to mention that your memories will be with us on the 27th too.

I have invited everyone to our house on 10th Muharram. We will collectively make special supplication for your success in the hereafter and try to make this day memorable.

11th December 2010

Adam, I hope you remember my old school friend from Pakistan? She called me yesterday. Her three-year-old son died. The funeral was today after the midday prayer. I went there with Daddy. There was another funeral of a baby girl. The funeral prayer of both the children was held in the same mosque.

The little boy had died suddenly. I saw his face inside the coffin Thanks be to the Almighty for he was a very cute child. It seemed as if he was smiling. I also saw the casket of the baby girl. She was very small and died only eighteen hours after her birth. Her name and age were written on the box "eighteen hours". At once, your gravestone flashed through my mind where your age of eighteen years was written. I thought it is Allah (SWT)'s Will that he grants an age of eighteen hours to some and eighteen years to others. Allah (SWT) has created every human being for a purpose.

He is God almighty. He grants as long a life to every person as He wishes. He has the control to grant either a short or long life. It seems to me that God reveals signs of His power to His people.

I had never seen the dead body of such a small baby. I met a lady there who was weeping bitterly and seemed very distressed. She told me that last year her teenage son died suddenly. We both sympathised with one another.

Today, I understood another reality which is absolutely true. When we perceive someone's sorrow and weep or express grief, we actually cry for our own misery. No one cries for others. All the people that I met today were crying due to their own grief. This lady was crying for her son. The mother whose son had died was yearning and crying for him and the tears which were falling from my eyes, Adam, were for you. Maybe now I can say that I can understand my friend's heartache because her grief and mine are the same.

Both the mothers' sorrows are similar. Both are mourning their sons. Whenever I go to a funeral, I get depressed because I think of you, your face, your coffin and your departure. Occasions like these rekindle my pain.

13th December 2010

These days I write regularly. My endeavour to convert my diary into a book form entails re-writing the whole thing. I am also working on the message which I wish to convey to people through this book.

I know this decision of mine will cause me pain. When I wrote the diary, I did not read it or correct it, but now when I started reading it again, I realise the pain and misery I went through.

This book will be no ordinary book for me. It will be like my own child in which I would see you. My dearest son Adam will be in this book; right from his birth until his departure from this world. This book is my love, my prayers, my grief and a road to a new life.

I do not need any fame or profit from this book. Any money that I collect through this book will be spent in charity work to be a source of eternal reward for my Adam and also for those people who buy this book. I want to show the same light of guidance to other people that I saw myself. I want them to experience the same fragrance that I did.

I pray to Allah (SWT) that all who read this book may be able to see the open doors which lead to our Creator.

I wish that these readers become my companions on this journey which will, God willing, lead us all to our final destination in the hereafter. Adam, God willing that is the place where I will meet you now.

15th December 2010

Adam, today is 9th Muharram. We are all fasting today. I am reliving last year's 9th Muharram.

It was Saturday. You got up late in the morning. You could not eat or drink anything. You said you were hungry but you also had tummy ache. Do you remember Adam that Uncle Abid, Auntie Zeenat and the children came to visit you? At iftaari (breaking of fast), Mamoon Mohammed, Auntie Erum and their children also came to see you. Even now, when I look at the empty sofa placed near the window, my eyes fill with tears. Just before going to the hospital on that day, you were lying on the same sofa watching the football match. I was frying samosas for the ending of the fast meal. Ambar, Arslan and Ahmad were making preparations for baking. I remember it all, Adam. I haven't forgotten anything and neither will I be able to forget it, ever. Those memories and that day have been engraved on my heart forever.

My dearest child that was your life's last day -9th Muharram when you were alive. Today I finished my office work early because I had to do some shopping for tomorrow. I have invited everyone to our house, for 10th Muharram, so that we can all pray for your forgiveness.

Before picking the children up from school today, I came to visit you at your residence; that is, the graveyard. I know I will not be able to come tomorrow. I wanted to visit you alone so that I could assess my own feelings. My eyes were filled with tears since morning. Though I was trying to be strong, still I could not stop the tears.

Before this, Adam, I had no association with tears. Now they have become a good friend of mine. I feel light and relieved after shedding tears.

As I was telling you, Adam, my heart was grief-stricken since morning, but surprisingly, when I reached your grave, I was in a strange frame of mind. I kept staring at the grave for quite some time. Not one tear dropped from my eyes, as if I was petrified.

I have begun to feel that now I do not know how I will react in a particular situation. Just like today, where I was expecting myself to break down completely, Allah (SWT) gave me a lot of strength. I began to meditate at your grave in silence. Today, I saw the graveyard in a completely different perspective.

The stone on your grave showed the date, 27th December 2009. 2010 began four days later. Now 2011 will begin after sixteen days. Time is like a runaway horse. I have begun to fear its speed.

Adam, the gravestones around you reveal the different ages of their inmates, like eighteen, nineteen, seventy-eight, sixty-eight, sixty-nine, seventy-two, fifty-four, fifty-eight, seventy-five, and some are graves of very small children. Written on one stone: age one hundred and two years. Every grave has different relations buried in them like son, husband, daughter, wife, sister, grandmother or grandfather, or maybe somebody's best friend.

I think this life is God's blessing. He grants each one of us as much as He wills. Some people are blessed with a long life and others get a short one.

The graveyard was deserted. This desolation always strikes me because there is a main road next to the cemetery. The stark contrast between the two is very obvious. On one side is this world with all its gaiety, restlessness, rushing about, impatience and gathering of people. On the other hand, one finds silence, serenity, leisure, loneliness and patience. What a contrast between the two worlds. People often remark that life is involvement, work and socialising, but when life ends, there is neither work, involvement nor friendship, only isolation and tranquillity. No doubt, all the activities of this world end for the person who dies.

Adam, today I closely observed the dilapidated building in the graveyard which often seems like a scene from a movie to me. I had always seen it from a distance. Today I got a chance to view it at close quarters. Its roof was in a very bad shape, the walls were very old and shabby and there were wooden boards nailed to its doors and windows. It looked like a skeleton of its former self which reminded me of a human skeleton. During life, the skeleton is covered with flesh and skin with pretty clothes donned over them. There is life and radiance on the face. But when the person dies, all that remains of him is a skeleton of bones. This is the system of nature.

As I was leaving the graveyard, I saw two labourers preparing someone's grave. Seeing them reminded me of the poet Wasi's couplet:

The grave is your final abode, at least make a bit of worship
One should not go empty handed to someone else's house.

16th December 2010 (7.10 a.m.)
10th Muharram

Today we all observed the fast of 10th Muharram. After the closing of the fast meal[1], everybody offered the pre-sunrise prayer and went to bed, but I was far away from sleep. My thoughts were focused on the previous year's 10th Muharram, when only one hour of my son's life in this world was left. My eyes were glued to the clock. Last year at this time Adam, you were about to leave us. We were all gathered around you. I tried to make you recite the Declaration of Faith (*Kalima*). You could not speak then, but I feel that you recited it many times in your heart.

Adam, I have realised that time is a very powerful element. The importance of time which has been revealed to me now, I could not understand before. I wish we would all respect time, that we should comprehend the importance of the hours and minutes left for us. But despite my wish I could not do anything. I was totally helpless before time.

Last year, we could not fast on 10th Muharram. The whole night we were with you in the hospital because the doctor had asked us to have family time with you. You were about to leave forever. None of us could fast in such circumstances.

I am not well today, either. I have got renal pain. Maybe it is some sort of infection, but the truth is that it is my heart which hurts me more than my kidney. When the pain stabs my heart, it leaves me gasping. It is so very intense that my whole being aches with it and tears fall non-stop from my eyes.

I think of your face. Your eyes were open. Your expression scared me. The pain and desolation in your eyes will haunt

---

1   The last meal to be eaten before the fast begins at the time of Fajr prayer.

me forever. Now I understand; that was the time you were leaving us and this world. Your eyes were not looking at me, they were looking at those angels who had come to take you.

An unknown poet wrote of this:

> *There was a strange pain in his eyes at the last hour*
> *It would make me grieve for him all my life.*

God has made the bond between mother and child so strong that no other relationship can compete with it. But God's love for us is seventy times more than a mother's love for her child. It is this fact which gives comfort to me. I know, Adam that you have gone to a far better place than this world. May God keep you in His protection (Ameen).

What a strange coincidence, Adam, that while writing today, I realised that only a few pages are left in this diary. It is almost as if the pages of this notebook also know that we are nearing the end of our journey.

Today, all the family members came to our house for your sake. Your Baba had composed a collective prayer for you. Later, we had dinner together. Then your maternal grandparents and other relatives called from Pakistan. Uncle Babur also called. Everyone showered you with prayers. Auntie Zeenat brought a very pretty bouquet of flowers. I hope you remember, Adam, that I loved flowers. I used to buy them for myself and also insisted on Daddy bringing them for me.

But now my perspective of this world and worldly things has changed completely. Everything seems trivial and small. The only things which have importance are people and our good deeds. Nothing is more important than these things. I still like flowers, but I will neither ask Daddy to bring flowers for me nor will I be upset if he does not.

Flowers

What does a flower know of its fate?
Whether it will be part of a bouquet
Or be trodden upon by people's feet

What does a flower know of its fate?
Whether it will be part of a garland of a groom
Or form a bracelet for a fair one
What does a flower know of its fate?
Whether it will convey condolences
Or congratulations

What does a flower know of its fate?
Whether it will wait to come to full bloom
Or will die before that
The same is the case of the people
They, too, enjoy life like a flower
Some live long lives, some die young

Every flower is pretty, every colour exquisite
Their fragrance is eternal, their variety is uncountable

Adam was a flower of my garden
He was dearer to me than the whole garden
May Allah protect my flower now
And grant me patience. May my garden bloom forever.
(Ameen)

(Urfana Ayub)

Adam, your Dadi Ammi thinks that I am not really ill. It is only the grief of being separated from you that has caused me to fall ill. My mother is also of the same view because she said,

"I think the cause of your illness is separation from your son."

When I went to visit your Dadi Ammi she sympathised with me and comforted me. She also told me not to cry, although she herself cries more than I do. Whenever she talks of you and remembers you, she invariably makes me cry, too.

Adam, these are things which cannot be told. These are sentiments and emotions which express themselves in many ways. Tears are also not under anybody's control. No doubt, the heart feels calm after tears.

19. The First Anniversary

19th December 2010

Adam, the children's Christmas holidays have begun. I hope you remember that last year, I took a fortnight's leave from my work and spent time with you.

It is the same time of year once again. This winter too, I have taken two weeks' holidays to be with the children. It is snowing heavily outside. The same vacations, the same snow, but this time without you.

20th December 2010

Man faces so many tests during his lifetime, different types of tests. Each trial seems like a mountain to the person challenged with it. What I have learnt from life is that Allah (SWT) observes His people, especially how they react in trying times, and whether they succeed in these tests set by Him or not. If they succeed, then there is reward for them. The bigger the test, the bigger the reward. Adam, no one can get a degree after nursery class. Allah (SWT) is never unjust to anyone.

I met a friend who is passing through a difficult phase in life and is very upset. God has subjected her to a tough test also. When a pivotal person of your life goes away it is like the death of that relationship. My friend is also facing a similar situation. Though no one has died, an important relationship has broken. More important than that, her trust has been eached and her heart has silently shattered into many pieces.

Adam, I sympathised with my friend and tried to make her strong. I explained to her that Allah (SWT) is subjecting her to a test. She should face it with courage and wait for Allah (SWT)'s reward.

23rd December 2010

Adam, today we all came to meet you. The whole graveyard was covered with snow. An eerie silence and desolation hung in the air. Everything was white as far as I could see.

The graves seemed very graceful against a white background. Yours was also covered with snow. A sense of grief overpowered me and I cried bitterly thinking of last year when I had come to the graveyard for the first time and saw your snow-covered grave.

After that, we went to Dadi Ammi's house because she had insisted that I take the children to her place for a few days during the Christmas holidays. We stayed there for three days. We talked a lot about you and wept in our grief.

I spent the night in the same room where I had stayed at Dadi Ammi's house immediately after your funeral. When I lay down on the bed, all the events of last year flashed through my mind, and today, one year later, I am again in the same room.

Adam, another coincidence is that we had never stayed at your grandmother's house before your departure, but after that we have stayed here twice. Today, Dadi Ammi told me someone's newborn baby suddenly died after he was brought home from hospital. The infant was normal and healthy. He went to sleep one night but never woke up. I wonder what that young woman's feelings would be who had become a mother for the first time. Sudden deaths are excruciatingly painful for the near and dear ones. May God grant patience to the baby's relatives (Ameen).

All praise be to God for you spent almost nineteen years of life with me, and your departure from this world has helped me see this life in a completely different perspective that enlightened my mind to the hereafter and increased my awareness of it. We are all thankful to God that He made you a part of our lives.

Adam, whenever I come to Dadi Ammi's house, she talks about you and yearns for you. Her feelings for you are very intense. She breaks down at every little memory of yours. I never knew she loved you so much. Your grandparents and everyone else have supported me immensely and helped me bear your loss.

May Allah (SWT) grant patience to them all and make them meet you in the highest heaven.

Last night, I went to Auntie Raheela's house. All the children were watching television. The room seemed empty, incomplete to me. I counted the children and asked where the rest of them were. They replied that all of them were present there. I counted again. All of my three children were there and so were Auntie Raheela's. Then suddenly, it dawned on me and my eyes filled with tears.

Yes Adam, there was somebody missing... That was you!

I often experience this feeling of someone missing while working in the kitchen, laying the table, etc. The departure of just one person makes the family look so small.

I realise one of my children has gone away. Previously, when somebody asked me about my children, I proudly answered, "Thank God I have four children." Now it is not so. The emptiness that is in my being is far more than what can be seen on the outside. Adam, I spent three memorable days with your Dadi Ammi, reminiscing and talking about you. She sent you all her love and prayers.

Many happy and sad memories are associated with this house. I brought you in this house after your birth, you grew up here and your last rituals were also held in this house. I feel, Adam, that after you, my relationship with other family members have strengthened somehow. Maybe we have started giving more importance to others. Here I received lots of love, courage, support and comfort from your grandparents, your Phuphie, and other family members. This love and support was so complete that I never missed my own parents and brothers. My heartfelt prayers are for all the family. This house has now become as though it were my own parents' house.

25th December 2010

Adam, it is Christmas today. Remember last year we spent the whole day at Dadi Ammi's house? Your cousin Huma is six years old today. I was debating whether to go to Uncle Yousaf's house or not for her party. This decision was difficult because I did not know how I would react, as last year you went there with us. We decided to go, but I cried all the way. I kept looking at the sky, trying to locate your name in the stars. When I reached your grandmother's place and met Dadi

Ammi, I could not hold back my tears.

After that, we went to Uncle Yousaf's house. My gaze was fixed on that sofa where you sat last year. Uncle Yousaf was sitting on one side and another child was sitting at the other end. The seat in the middle was empty. This was the very place where you had sat silently last year with your head bowed because your stomach was in pain.

Not seeing you on that sofa and in the room was very distressing for me. You are now only in my heart and memories. After a while, your grandfather came into the room and sat in the same place where he had sat last year. His eyes were filled with tears. Maybe he was thinking the same thing that was going through my mind. Adam, you have no idea how much your grandfather has loved you. There are very few grandfathers like yours. He has superbly fulfilled all the obligations of a grandfather right from your birth until your burial. He always loved you like his son. He caressed you, took you to nursery and happily did all the little chores for you. I know that he is heartbroken but he is concealing his sorrow from everyone around him.

He misses you immensely and often remarks, "When I fell ill in Pakistan, Adam brought me to England." You were a lucky boy Adam, because you received love from every relation of yours. You were the first to make them grandparents, you were their first grandchild, and you also made your maternal grandparents into grandparents for the first time. You gave every one of us a new family member for the very first time.

Though you spent a very limited time with your siblings, in my eyes you will always be Taya Abbu (elder brother of father) for Arslan and Ahmad's children. I will introduce all the brides, grooms and children who come into this family to you. I will explain their relationship with you. I have lovingly preserved all the things associated with you that I could, and I will show these things to all the children of the family. You are alive in all your relationships, whether with people who are here now or with those to come.

Today, I talked to my mother in Pakistan. She told me that my brother Atif had an accident. Praise be to God who saved his life. An unknown woman immediately took him to hospital where medical aid was provided. In return for her support, that lady only asked for prayers. This made me realise that there are still good people around. That woman came as a blessing for us, otherwise anything could have happened.

26th December 2010

This morning on Auntie Uzmah's radio programme, I requested her to play a song which always reminds me of you, whose every word reflects my sentiments.

He was like blowing wind
He was like a flying kite
Where can I find him?

It is almost as if the writer wrote this song especially for you.

Today, we went to the graveyard to visit you. Your grave was still covered with snow. Every passing minute was reminding me of last year's 26th December.

This sequence of memories started as soon as I woke up. I remember last year you slept in my room. It was about the time of the sunset prayer when you were lying on the sofa watching a football match on TV. Then you got ready to go to hospital, and I remember everything about your check-up in the hospital.

All praise be to Allah who has granted me so much patience. I put up a brave show throughout the day. I looked at your photographs, brought your first teddy bear to my room and caressed it. I talked to my parents. They sent their heartfelt prayers to you and reaffirmed their support for me. All the relatives in England also telephoned me, sent you their blessings and encouraged me to bear the loss with courage.

27th December 2010

Time
A time period has completed today
Many more time periods will pass, but you will not be here

These blowing winds, stars, the scenes, dawn and dusk
All whisper to me about your life's journey

The time period which was one year only
I lived many years in it

Moments changed to minutes and minutes to hours
I completed this journey from hours to a year

Now the years will pass remembering you
The universe will be the same but you will not be there

The thought of life without you is a torture
I will pass through many such tortures but you will not be here

A time period has completed today

Many more time periods will pass, but you will not be here
(Urfana Ayub)

December 16 2010
10th Muharram

Adam, I am confused as to how should I start writing today.

Maybe it is because a full year is complete today. I am surprised how my sentiments got translated into words and formed a full poem. Every word of this poem reflects my thoughts and feelings. "Many more time periods will pass, but you will not be here!" This is the truth.

This morning after offering the pre-sunrise prayer, I could not go back to sleep. I kept thinking that this time last year my son was alive; he was breathing. The seconds were passing and my eyes were glued to the wall clock and then it was 8.10 in the morning. I recited *"Indeed, we all belong to Allah and to Him shall we return"*, a Qur'anic verse.

It was a very strange feeling. There are so many sentiments to which you cannot put a name, a title. You can simply describe them as strange. I too can call it strange only. Maybe there is no word for it in a dictionary, either. We all prayed for your forgiveness again and supplicated to Allah (SWT). While I was engaged in prayer, somebody called on the telephone. It was from Dadi Ammi's friend's house to tell us that her husband passed away in the morning.

This got me thinking that exactly one year after you, Adam, another person departed from this world that was known to me. Thousands of people come to this world daily and thousands go away. These births and deaths are not restricted by days or months. It is the same seven days of the week and the same twelve months of the year. This is God's nature's system.

Adam, another odd feeling is that since you went away, it seems that more people have started dying. This is not actually so. People died before, too, but I did not perceive death. Now I have become more aware of death, and it seems that someone is dying every other day.

Adam, I have some good news for you today! Daddy bought a new car! If you were here, you would have been very pleased to see it. But if you ask me the make or model of the car, do you think I would know it? Of course not! You know very well that I have no interest in cars. For your information the new car is dark blue in colour. That's my level of knowledge in cars.

I was upset when your father told me he wanted to sell his seven-seater car. We had very fondly bought this car a few years back because, thanks be to God, we were six family members who did not fit in an ordinary family saloon car.

Now that you are not here anymore, Daddy says we do not need a big car. An ordinary car will do. This is true because now, whenever we go out as a family, the two back seats remain vacant. These empty seats make me sadder.

Adam, all the family telephoned me today and offered their sympathy and support once more. Many friends sent text messages expressing their love and empathy for us. My parents phoned from Pakistan. All my brothers sent their love and prayers from Pakistan. All these relatives have not even seen your grave.

In the evening, your Daddy and I went to Dadi Ammi's friend's house whose husband had died. We offered prayers for his forgiveness. The ladies were reciting the Holy Text and Surah Yaseen (chapter of Qur'an). Many were reciting the Declaration of Faith on rosary beads, and again, last year's 27th December started playing in my mind like a film. I prayed for the forgiveness of the deceased.

At night, Adam, three of your friends, Amir, Abdullah and Umar, came to our house. They had remembered the date. First they phoned your father and then came to our home. I had spent the whole day with a lot of composure and courage, but when your friends came and started talking to your father about football I could not fight my tears anymore.

I showed them your first teddy bear which was actually a gift for your first birthday, and also your first babygrow that Dadi Ammi had given me. I sat with them for some time, but my patience wore out and I got up before my tears could betray my emotions and went to my room. The boys kept talking to your Daddy and Arslan for quite some time.

Adam, Arslan has matured a lot this year and has become very sensible. When I went up to my room at night and wept, he sensed my agony and came upstairs to me. He silently hugged me and kept standing with me, which gave me a lot of courage and strength. Do you know what I told him?

"Arslan, you are my Adam and you are my Arslan."

Ever since I have started writing my diary, I feel very light. I simply write what I feel, but gradually I noticed a change in my style of writing. I automatically started addressing you in my writing. I think this change came over during my pilgrimage journey.

Then, as 27th December approached, I felt a restlessness and anxiety in me. I was nearing the end of a time period; an era.

I contemplated whether I should keep writing my diary and talking to you for the rest of my life or whether I should make this diary useful for other people, too. I finally decided to stop writing the diary after today, 27th December 2010. This was not an easy decision for me. I had recorded my feelings and events of the whole year in this journal.

Every positive act is difficult, Adam. The truth is that you are gone. Even if I keep awake the whole night and spend the days pining and grieving for you, if I keep writing my diary and distance myself from this world and waste my abilities, I will not be helping anyone in this way.

I have a fervent desire to convert my diary into a book and publish it. Through this book I want to convey my message to all those mothers who, like myself, have lost their sons. No, not lost; I think the most appropriate term is bade farewell. It is for all the mothers, sisters, daughters, fathers, brothers, sons, husbands and wives who have also bade farewell to their dear ones.

I am not a writer and I do not have any experience of writing either. I am surprised that I, who had never written a verse in my life, could compose poems like "I Don't Know Where He Is Lost" and "Time".

Adam, please pray that this book may be a source of eternal reward for you and may it change the thinking, perceptions and lives of all those who read it. May God help me complete this project and accept my endeavours, Ameen.

I don't know how I will feel once it hits home that I will not

156

be writing my diary anymore. I am trying to make myself understand that Allah (SWT) expects many other tasks from me. You had to go away from this world. It is a fact! It is better to come out of the dreams and face reality. Being realistic saves us from many complications.

The publishing of this book will be like the rebirth of Adam. I feel that I am passing through the agony of creation once more. I will always sense you in this book.

Adam, my next meeting with you will be in the book, which I will call "After You Were Gone". But if I can't wait that long, then maybe I will write a letter to you, especially on the occasion of Arslan, Ambar and Ahmad's weddings. During all these events, it will be difficult for me to keep my emotions under control. Please God give me courage that I may remain strong on all these occasions. So many people are praying for you. So many hearts are wishing well for you. You are a lucky individual, Adam, because you received love from so many people.

You received lots of respect and status. You, too, respected and loved everyone.

The truth is, your departure from this world has had a positive impact on the lives of people around you. Many severed relationships were mended and people began thinking of Allah (SWT), their grave and the Day of Reckoning, praise be to Allah (SWT).

My dear son, I will bid you farewell once again amidst my heartiest prayers. May Allah (SWT) protect you always, my child, and save you from the torments of the grave. If deliberately or unknowingly you made any mistake in your short life, may Allah (SWT) pardon you by His grace and everlasting mercy.

Oh God, please place my son in the highest level of heaven. Let his grave be one of the gardens of heaven. If there were any shortcomings in his prayers (*Ibaadah*), please pardon him for it. Oh God let me meet my son one day. Help me live my life with courage and patience (Ameen).

May you shine like a moon and live among the stars
May you spread your fragrance like a flower and be respected in the world

Adam, your life in this world was like a flower which spread beautiful scent around it and faded away. You are the first flower of my garden.

Dadi Ammi says, "Adam was the most precious flower of my garden." Now I pray that "May you shine like a moon and live among the stars." Whenever I look at the sky, I can see your name written there by the stars. May Allah (SWT) be your Guardian. Allah Hafiz

20. My Message

إِنَّ اللَّهَ مَعَ الصَّابِرِينَ

Verily, Allah (SWT) is with those who patiently persevere.
(Al-Baqarah, 153)

Life is the most precious of God's blessings, but we are not aware of its value. We should meditate on life and try to find out the reason for our creation. We tend to forget that everything has a purpose. Likewise, God has a motive behind the creation of mankind.

Just think about this life which has been granted to us by God. Why did He give it to us? What does God want from us?

You will not have to go to any library to find answers to these questions. Simply ask yourself. If you still do not understand, seek help from the holy Qur'an which is the last book of Allah (SWT). Try to maintain a connection, a hotline with Allah (SWT). Make an effort to understand and get closer to your Creator. You will find answers to all your queries.

Make friends with the holy Qur'an by reading and understanding it. You will realise that no friend is more faithful and truthful than this because, like a sincere friend, it will give you the best advice regarding every aspect of life. That advice will be beneficial to you at each stage of life, and in your relationship with the world, religion and the Hereafter. This is the one and only path that will lead you to your chosen destination, God willing.

Whenever we want to seek advice from someone, we choose our most trusted friend or relative because we believe they will not betray us. It is human nature to trust others. Usually, people who think alike can become friends and the bond of friendship between them is formed. In such cases, there is some common factor like similar likes, language, thinking or country which binds them together.

We require words to form a relationship. Thus, language is fundamental. If we want to be friends with the Qur'an, it is imperative that we understand its meaning.

If we do not understand our friend's language, how will we comprehend his message? Our friendship will not prosper. We will not benefit from it as much as we should. The same is the case of the Muslim Ummah today. We simply recite the Qur'an in arabic without understanding and are satisfied that we have fulfilled our duty. We have done worship. We feel content having recited one section of the Qur'an at a time or reciting the Qur'an three times during the month of Ramadhan.

Ask yourself whether you understood a single page or even one verse of it? If the answer is "yes", then God bless you, for you are lucky to have reached the stage where you can understand some of the Qur'an.

But if your answer is "no", then it is something for you to worry about, because all of God's instructions, whether of small or large magnitude, are present in this Qur'an.

It is my request to all those who read this book that if you have not read the Qur'an with understanding; that is, translated into your own language, or with a knowledge of arabic, then please make up your mind to do so. If you already know its meaning, then make an effort to understand it and act upon it. Read it again and again. Try to attend Qur'an classes which will help you comprehend the message of the Qur'an.

Amend and rectify your ways and deeds according to God's instructions. What has been done up until now is done. Nothing is lost yet. Make a new beginning. Repent of your shortcomings and ask God almighty for His forgiveness. Every day is a new beginning. Start each day by thanking him for His blessings and living your life according to the guidelines set by our Creator.

The death of my son has strengthened my faith. It has clarified the actual meaning of life and death. Observing death from such close quarters was a powerful learning experience for me.

I have finally realised that if this is life, then there is very little which is in our power. Man is very weak. All the world's riches, respect and fame cannot buy a moment of life for anybody. And then I thought...

Why have we complicated our lives so much?
Why don't we spare time for others?
Why don't we have time even for our own selves?
Why is all our time spent only on worldly matters?
Where have we left our religion?

The very religion for which our beloved Prophet Muhammad (Peace Be Upon Him) faced so many hardships to spread.

What about the objective for which Allah (SWT) created us?
Is our conscience dead?
Who will bring it back to life? Is there anyone?

Allah (SWT) sent many messengers and holy books to educate mankind, but no one will come now! Allah (SWT) conveyed his complete message to us in His last revelation - the Holy Qur'an and promised to preserve it, so that no man could corrupt it.

When one fully comprehends the purpose of his own creation, then he or she will not waste his abilities or incapacitate himself by the grief of a loved one's death. He knows that this world and man himself is finite. Everyone has to go, one after the other. This fact comforted me.

What is life?

I have understood that we spend very little time in this world. Then we will die and go into our eternal life. We are so engrossed in this life that we forget we have to go away ultimately.

By God's standards, the criterion for success is not property, a thriving business, the latest model car or a huge bank balance.

I have understood the meaning of mankind's success. Ever since I grasped what life really is, everything of this world seems trivial, meaningless. I must make preparation for my success in the eternal life. I may be called upon any day to return back to Allah (SWT). This notion worries me. Whenever we have to go somewhere, we are anxious and we pack our belongings that we intend to take on the journey. There is a restlessness in us.

But alas! All this planning, anxiety and worry is for the journeys of this world only. Ask yourself! Isn't it true?

This realisation hit me when I experienced the sudden death of my teenaged son. He was very well dressed. He liked wearing trendy and expensive clothes.

But now that he is no more, the clothes are in his cupboard, the jackets, sweaters, shoes and other belongings, are lying lifeless where he left them. I realised that he did not take anything with him. Not even a finger ring, although it is very small. Man does not need any worldly thing for his departure except his burial shroud (kafan - clothing which the deceased is dressed in). Only our deeds, be they good or bad, travel with us to the Hereafter. This perception changed my thought process completely.

What is required and what is waste?

Where do I spend my time and how should it be spent?

Time is investment, in other words, money. I understand the value of time and at the same time I feel intimidated by it also. I could not prolong my son's life even by a moment. It was not in my power to do so.

We spend time without thinking of its power.

Sitting for hours on end in front of the television screen.

Talking for hours on the telephone.

Sometimes just sitting quietly without doing anything.

We do not realise that doing zikr, remembrance of Allah (SWT), or praying instead of sitting idle or wasting time in any other way will add credit to our good deeds. Who knows that just ten minutes' worship during these times may save us from hellfire in the hereafter.

My message is for all those mothers who lost their children - life is courage. One who is destined to go away will go, may that be Adam or someone of any other name. He who has gone will never come back.

God has not been unjust to you. The objective of that person's life was fulfilled so Allah summoned him back. One should not complain to God about it.

Always remember the devil is a sworn enemy of man. If he could make the Prophet Adam (AS) disobey Allah (SWT), then we are no match for him. Prophet Adam (AS) was the first man created. He was formed by Allah (SWT)'s command "Be", and he was created, not through parents. Allah (SWT) granted him abode in heaven as a favour and gave him fine clothes to wear. Satan has been man's enemy from the day one. He never wants man to pray to Allah (SWT) and be thankful to Him. He always creates doubts in the hearts of believers so that they disobey Allah (SWT).

Just like one is always alert to one's foes, similarly we should always beware of the devil, so that we may not fall into his trap and do something which displeases God. The grief of a loved one's death is very great. The deceased person can be any one of your relations, like a child, brother, sister, friend or other family member. It is all God's Will and His test for His people.

I have learnt that the qualities of patience and thankfulness go hand in hand and both are necessary. Allah has said in the Qur'an many times to seek help through patience and thankfulness because this is the path which will lead to success. No doubt they are difficult to practice, but we must also understand that we cannot earn a big reward for a small deed. To achieve big rewards from Allah (SWT), we have to do great deeds. One must pray to Allah (SWT) for this.

Initially, I also felt that I would suffocate from grief or my heart would rip apart due to sorrow. How would I live my life without my son? I am aware that my son no longer lives in my house. He does not sleep in the comfortable bed of his room. Rather, he has gone off to sleep in his mud-grave forever. This thought shakes me to the core. Whenever the weather changes and it snows, rains or is even sunny, I feel intensely that he is outside the shelter of his home.

But praise be to Allah (SWT) my sustainer who gave me the courage to bear it and much more besides. It is only Allah (SWT) who comforts people. I found answers to all my difficult questions and problems in my religion. All the questions relating to death which were bothering me, I tried to find their solution in the holy Qur'an and the teachings of Prophet Mohammed (Peace Be Upon Him). These teachings consist of all that the Prophet Mohammed (Peace Be Upon Him) was reported to have said, done, or permitted others to do.

The Qur'an repeatedly mentions the people who practice patience, and promises them heaven as their reward.

The second quality is that of gratitude. I realise that Allah (SWT) has blessed me with uncountable bounties such as my home, husband, healthy children, parents, sisters and brothers. In fact He has blessed me with every possible worldly comfort.

Out of all these blessings, I lost just one person. I admit he was a very beloved person, a part of my being, but he was one of the infinite bounties which Allah (SWT) had bestowed upon me.

I still have incalculable blessings of God with me. Have I become numb? Can't I see all the blessings of God? Who will thank Him for granting me so much? I felt ashamed. This feeling somewhat eased my sorrow. I am ever thankful to Allah (SWT) for granting me children. Where the Qur'an mentions the people who practice patience, it also speaks of people who are thankful to God.

Another important message I want to convey concerns Bid'at. At present, our society is engulfed with Bid'at.

What is Bid'at?

Any deed or action for which we find no reference in the Qur'an nor Sunnah, but which becomes a practice among people because they think that they will be rewarded for it or they simply copy it from others. Bid'at is an extra deed or routine which is not part of religion. It is commonly seen in many rituals practiced during weddings or deaths. It causes people to spend their time and money superficially; the Soyem (third day ritual after death) followed by the Chaleeswan on the fortieth day. Then, death anniversaries each year and the practice of observing grief on the first Eid after death. If all the money and time spent on these occasions is used instead in some constructive work with the intention of charity for the deceased's everlasting reward, it will benefit him or her.

Whenever you do something, ask yourself, "Am I obeying something stated in the Qur'an or Sunnah, or am I doing it just because it is a social practice?"

Do not make these Bid'at a part of your daily life only to please people. Your priority should be to please God almighty.

Our beloved Prophet Muhammad (SAW) said: "*There are two of Allah's bounties which most people do not value and tend to waste. One is health and the other is leisure.*" (Sahih Bukhari) – authentic collection of sayings and actions of Prophet Muhammad (Peace Be Upon Him).

It is a fact that people think they will always remain healthy.

166

They never think of making the most of their healthy time and offering worship least Allah (SWT) should take back His blessing of health and leave the person unable to even offer the daily obligatory prayer (*Salah*).

Similarly, leisure is also a special blessing of Allah (SWT). Life does not remain constant, so be thankful for the favours that have been bestowed upon you.

One thing which I have learned from my life and also from the experience of people around me is that anything can happen to you and also that your situation can change in a split second. One must always be prepared for both these things. Never boast about anything, whether in pride or otherwise.

Your actions or words may hurt someone's feelings. Allah (SWT) does not like boasting and He may punish you for it in this world or the hereafter. Always think the best of others. Do not doubt their intentions. This is absolutely necessary for success.

All praise be to God I have never thought ill or wished bad for others. I respect everyone. My intentions regarding others are also clear. But maybe I have hurt someone's feelings. After thinking carefully over it, I still think that I have tried my level best not to hurt anyone deliberately, but if I have unintentionally done so, then I humbly apologise to everyone through this book. I myself have forgiven everyone for Gods's sake; that is, anyone who may have wronged me. I pray that Allah (SWT) pardons my shortcomings and sins, also (Ameen).

If you do not understand something, then consider the fact that God is testing you. Don't let yourself be impatient or ungrateful to Allah in these trying situations.

Another important point towards which I want to draw every- one's attention – if God has given you a child who has any kind of physical or mental disability, never, ever consider him or her any less than other children. We say that society is unjust towards these "special" children. I think it is not society, but the child's own parents, siblings and other relatives who discriminate against him by pitying him.

If God has given you such a child, then take it as a test of your patience and thankfulness from God. Look for that extra gift in the child which Our Creator has bestowed upon him in lieu of his disability. Open your heart and mind to see the child's potential; otherwise, you will be committing injustice towards your child by not recognising the pearl that God has granted you. Respect and value these children because they can become a means for your forgiveness and good deeds.

Another very important message I wish to convey to my readers is to value your family and give them time. The relatives, for whom you earn money, build homes, buy cars and so many other worldly things also require that you spend time with them. Convey your feelings and emotions to these relatives. There are many people we respect, many relatives whom we love so much that we cannot think of a life without them, but still we do not express our feelings in words. I admit that true emotions like love and respect should not need the help of words for understanding, but still words play a pivotal role in keeping these bonds alive. Learn to express yourself.

Do not only point out your children's mistakes, try to find out their talents instead.

Realise the comforting protection that you enjoy from your

parents and tell them what you haven't been able to say until now. Express your love for your wife, husband or any other family member. Do not hold back thinking that they know already. Many times these words will add intensity and colour to relationships. Just like when the walls of a house begin to discolour and fade with time, a coat of paint will make them pretty once again.

Mend those connections which have broken or weakened due to misunderstanding, separation, lack of time or some other reason, because Allah (SWT) has said repeatedly in the Qur'an to do this and has allocated precious rewards for people who try to maintain relationships, strengthen bonds and mend broken links.

Whenever you embark on a journey, always see your parents before leaving and take their blessings with you. Your aim behind these actions should be that maybe you will not get a chance to meet them again; maybe you will die before then. My Adam's departure has given a new depth and dimension to this thought of mine. When he stepped out of the house for the last time, neither he nor I could have thought that these would be his last steps.

This idea still scares me even one year after his departure. It is proof that anyone can leave this world at any time. Consider every journey as your last one. Ask yourself at the end of each day whether you have hurt anyone. If intentionally or unintentionally any such incident has happened, then do not lose time to phone or text them, apologise and clear the air between yourselves. If it is your family members whom you have hurt, then sit with them face to face and remove any misunderstandings. Always be aware that it is the devil that causes disharmony and clashes. You must not let him succeed in this.

My husband and I often discuss the fact that if a person is ill, he has more chances of dying than a healthy person. I have total faith in the fact that it makes no difference to your chances of dying if you have a heart problem, diabetes, cancer or, God forbid, any other serious ailment.

When your destined time approaches, you have to go no matter what. I am surprised when, after someone's death, people contemplate that if he hadn't gone there, or if he hadn't travelled by train or if he hadn't done this, he might still be alive. In my opinion, no. No illness of the world can cause someone's death unless Allah (SWT) causes him to die. Similarly, even the healthiest of all men cannot live forever. Even with people who take full precautions regarding their health, I have heard of incidents where healthy people who never even suffered from even common cold, died suddenly in the gymnasium while exercising. It is all in God's power.

When someone dies, consider that the objective of his life was fulfilled. Try to make out what you learned from his life as well as his death.

What did Adam leave behind?

There are people in this world who are not able to achieve the things that get done in later years, because of their death at a young age. This was similar to my Adam's story. But when he was alive he showed love to every relative. His smile was famous everywhere. He won people over with a smile. His personality was affectionate; made up of precious and very beautiful qualities. He gave and received love.

My son was in a rush to leave this world. His death was sudden and he reached his final abode very quickly too. Everything happened so fast that even after his burial many people were asking, "When is the funeral? Did you receive his body"? I consider this all to be God's blessing, all praise be to God.

What did Adam do in his life?

- He shocked our world by his sudden death.
- He left many questions for people to ask themselves.
- What is the reality of life and death?
- He left a message for all youngsters.
- He distributed love amongst families.
- He left his identity behind.
- He left behind an example of patience and courage.
- He proved that he was the grandson of a soldier. My Abbu says every person is Allah's soldier. He bows his head before Allah (SWT) in the same manner as a worldly soldier bows before his officer.
- He left a message of patience for me because, when he was about to go, he wiped away my tears and signalled to his father and me not to cry.

The biggest favour he gave me was to make me see my own last abode. Though I have been living in this country for the last twenty years, I never had a chance to visit a graveyard. Seeing the graveyard and Adam's grave opened my eyes to a whole new world.

Sentiments from the Family

After the departure of my child, Adam Ayub, the whole family became more united. Secondly, everybody began thinking more of death, the grave, the hereafter and Allah (SWT). We came to the realisation that our stay in this world is very limited.

(Kulsoom - Adam's paternal grandmother)

Adam Ayub's death made us all a step closer to God. Now I love my children even more than before.

(Yaqoob - Adam's paternal grandfather)

After Adam's death, I have focussed my full attention towards religion because I know that only this will benefit me in the end. I want to spend quality time remembering and thanking Allah (SWT).

(Erum – Adam's maternal uncle's wife)

I have learnt that Allah (SWT) is the Almighty and Most Powerful. We are unable to do anything against His Will. We have to be patient under all circumstances.

(Arshia – Adam's paternal uncle's wife)

After Adam, I have begun to think that life is very short and I have started getting closer to God.

(Raheela – Adam's paternal uncle's wife)

As an unknown poet said:

He left in such a manner that the whole weather pattern

172

changed
The departure of just one person made the town deserted
(Tayyaba - Auntie)

I have become acutely aware of the fact that life is very short. No one knows when it will end. Try to be as good to others as you can, so that they may think well of you. Everyone must make preparation for the Hereafter.

(Mohmmed – Adam's maternal uncle)

Adam always seemed to us like our son Zakaria. He was a very good-natured boy who loved and cared for others. He is alive in our hearts and will always remain so. His loss has left this world deficient of a very kind person. His birth meant we became someone's maternal uncle and aunt (in-law) for the first time. We have no words which can do justice to our emotions that we are feeling after his death.

His departure also made us realise that we miss our relatives more so when they have gone far away from us. His smiling face will always be in our special thoughts. We pray to Allah (SWT) to put him in the highest levels of Heaven and give patience to all his relatives, Ameen.

(Kaleem - Adam's maternal uncle & Humaira – Kaleem's wife)

After Adam, we felt as if our own child had left us. Adam was a kind boy who was very respectful and always obedient towards all his elders. He loved all his relatives. No one can replace him. His departure has left a void which cannot be filled. His smiling face is always in our hearts. Words cannot describe the pain and sorrow of his parents who have lost such an intelligent and a fine boy. May Allah (SWT) give him an abode in Heaven, and may He grant patience to all of us, Ameen.

(Kashif - Adam's maternal uncle & Azra – Kashif's wife)

173

This world is finite and we all have to go beyond it. This fact became clearer after Adam, and I have realised that we should be more worried and make more preparations for the Hereafter than we do for this world.

(Atif – Adam's maternal uncle)

I have become acutely aware of two things after Adam. Firstly, that "man is like a traveller in this world". He will leave all his worldly belongings here. The only things which will go forward with him are good deeds.

Secondly, "the bird will fly away leaving the empty cage behind". Just like a traveller or a bird, Adam went away from this world. The world's houses and rooms were left behind vacant, like those cages where birds used to live like in a home. There is Allah's message in it for us all, if only we can decipher it. He has gone leaving his room empty, but he is and will always, remain alive in our hearts. May God increase his degrees in heaven and give patience to us, Ameen.

(Fauzia – Adam's maternal uncle's wife)

May Allah (SWT) bless you with the highest ranks in Paradise, and may He make you a means of blessings and Heaven for your parents. Your absence will be felt by those you left behind all their lives. You were a very fine person who loved and respected others. Your vibrant smile and expressive shiny eyes will always be in our hearts. I miss you very much and think of you. May God elevate your ranks and make everything easy for you. May Allah (SWT) shower his hospitality on you according to His Grace, Ameen.

(Ishaque - Adam's maternal grandfather)

After Adam, it seemed as if my child has gone away. I, too, have to travel down this road because death is definite. The time of death cannot be moved forward nor backward by even a moment. Everything has to perish. I must try to speed up my preparations for the Hereafter. I feel my child's absence all the time. His smiling eyes and face is always in my thoughts.

"O beloved one, my hands which I raised to Allah to pray for your health and long life will now be raised to ask for your forgiveness.

"O Lord, bless my child with Heaven and place him in higher levels of Heaven. O Allah (SWT), entertain him according to Your Grace and forgive all his shortcomings and mistakes, Ameen."

O dear Adam
You have gone where we all have to travel
You have gone towards your Creator's blessings
(Zahida Nasreen)

Death is the greatest blessing. It is the biggest truth of life. It liberates man from the miseries and sorrows of life and makes him closer to Allah (SWT). It gives us cause to worry and prepare ourselves for the Hereafter. It is not bound by time. Ehsan Danish talks about death in the following words:

The frames of the grave are vacant, do not forget them
Whose picture will be posted, and when, nobody knows

Adam was like a heartbeat for everyone, a very loving child and my first grandson. No one can take his place. He is with us in our hearts, eyes, mind, emotions and prayers and will always remain so. His death has exalted him. He is sorely missed by everyone. His personality was such that all his near and dear ones were sorrowful for him; all the eyes were moist with his memories. Zahid Fateh Puri's following couplet describes Adam's personality:

Live your life in such a way That even those who tend to forget

175

will remember you all their lives
(Zahida - Adam's maternal grandmother)

May Allah (SWT) bless you with the highest ranks in Paradise, and may He make you a means of blessings and Heaven for your parents. Your absence will be felt by those you left behind all their lives. You were a very fine person who loved and respected others. Your vibrant smile and expressive shiny eyes will always be in our hearts. I miss you very much and think of you. May God elevate your ranks and make everything easy for you. May Allah (SWT) shower his hospitality on you according to His Grace, Ameen.

(Zahida Nasreen - Adam's maternal grandmother)

Messages from the original edition of this book

This book was originally published in the Urdu language in April 2011. The following thoughts and memories from family members and friends appeared in the English Section within that book. They are reproduced here.

My Brother

Adam Ayub (07/05/1991 – 27/12/2009)

On the 27th of March 1994 in the afternoon I opened my eyes in the Bradford Royal Infirmary hospital where I met my mum, dad and my elder brother Adam Ayub for the very first time. He was very excited and happy to see me with a huge smiling grin on his face. He was three years old at that time. I used to play and fight with him all the time, just like two close brothers would do. He would protect and guide me all the time. I remember him going to hospital regularly, but at that time I was not aware of his health conditions.

He was a happy child and was very special to all the family due to the fact he was the first grandchild of the two families of our parents. When he was five years old he went through major heart surgery and I heard everyone was praying for his health and wellbeing. The surgery that he went through was life threatening and complex. He was in Intensive Care for a long time after his heart operation, and everyone was pleased when he came home.

He grew up to be a very lovely, confident, kind and polite person. We used to go to the same primary school, Bradford Moor Primary School, during the day and in the evening to Madni Masjid (mosque) where we went for our religious education. I had a very special bond with him from my early age, since we were the only two boys of the family at that time. During the years of being at primary school and beginning secondary school, he was regularly monitored by heart specialists at Leeds General Infirmary. He used to go for regular check-ups but he was growing well and doing well with his studies at school.

Over the years I went to Pakistan with Adam and our family for our uncle's wedding and we went to see different parts of Pakistan and spend time with our extended family. I have many lovely cherished moments of us in Pakistan in photographs and many videos which got taken by our mum. We had a fantastic time there and Adam always loved going; he wanted to go every year back to Pakistan if he could. We really loved meeting my mother's family, the hot weather, the beach, the attention and love we used to get from the family.

After finishing school successfully, he went for Umrah (religious pilgrimage) in Saudi Arabia and then went to Pakistan to see all the family there. We were all very proud of him, as he was the first grandchild to go to college. Everyone was overjoyed for him. Adam went to Bradford College to do his A-Levels in Business and Computing. In college he met new people and made new friends, but I knew I was his very best friend and brother. This was because he used to tell me all his secrets and all the new things that he was up to.

Adam and I had the same interests and hobbies. Adam was really interested in football from a very young age, probably because our dad and uncles played all the time. He also had met all the England football team and had his photograph taken with them. We went to watch Arsenal, Manchester United, Real Madrid, and Juventus two years ago at the Emirates Stadium in London. It was a very memorable day out for all of us. We took some pictures of all of us fooling around.

We had many family trips like going in Holland, Pakistan, Saudi Arabia. The last holiday we both went together on was in August 2009. We went to Egypt (Sharm el Sheikh) and had a very memorable holiday, but I never thought that would be the last time we would go on holiday together. We were planning to go to Saudi Arabia and then Pakistan in the summer holidays of 2010 as a family.

In September 2009 Adam started at Leeds Metropolitan University and started doing a Youth and Community Degree for three years. This was one of the happiest moments for my parents, and us all as a family; the first and most special child of the family started University. He started off very well since he got really good grades in his first assignment. He was happy as well.

During this time his health was deteriorating and he was getting irregular heartbeats, which were causing him problems, and having minor operations. He was in and out of hospitals on a regular basis for check-ups and treatments. His heart was getting weak. In October 2009 we were supposed to go to Bruges in Belgium as a family, but we missed the ferry and it was booked again for December (Christmas Holidays). Adam was not feeling well in December so he didn't go; our mum stayed with him at home to look after him.

He was unwell for the first two weeks of December; his appetite was not good. He was vomiting and he had really bad stomach pains. My mum took time off work to spend the school holidays with us. We watched family movies and our parents' wedding movie together.

On Christmas we went to grandma's house and we spent the whole day there with our family and also attended our cousin's sister's birthday party. He was unwell that day and went to the walk-in surgery. On Saturday 26th of December 2009 my parents took him to LGI for a check-up. When he was going we said bye to him and Mum said, "We will be back in a couple of hours".

I never imagined that these would be his last steps in our house and he would never be able to set foot in this house again. I remember Mum called me to say that they have taken Adam to the ward to get checked. It was two in the morning when my uncle took us to the hospital to see Adam. He was diagnosed with pneumonia and the doctors said that he will not be able to get through this. I was in shock when I heard this; I thought he was going to come back after his check-up.

When I went to hospital and I saw his face, I started to cry, as I couldn't believe he was going. He was unconscious and he had an oxygen mask on but I spoke to him. I told him how much I love him and I asked him for forgiveness for any wrongdoings I had done to him. My whole family was surrounding his bed. My mum and dad were also crying. Me, my youngest brother and sister, were still confused and were not sure what was happening as it happened all of a sudden. I could not believe it.

I went to my grandmother's house with my brother and sister and we were all praying for his life. Everyone was praying for him. After about two hours we went back to the hospital, but on the way my dad called and said "he has passed away". When we got there and I saw his body, I was so devastated that he has gone. Words can't explain how I felt.

His funeral and burial happened on the same day. He left me with many memories of a lifetime. I still cannot believe he is gone. I miss the time we had spent together, our laughs, fights, good times, bad times, him annoying me etc.

I hope he has gone to heaven and hope that I can meet him one day. I miss him every day and love him a lot. He will stay in my heart all the time. He was and always will be my brother and my best friend. I love you Adam Ayub (Rest in peace). Ameen.

Arslan Ayub (Younger brother)

Adam

Your smile was catching I miss your smile
Your smile was a candle in my life just like your eyes
Your eyes were sparkling I miss your eyes
Your eyes had life the life of hope
I will keep the hope for the rest of my life
I wish you rest in peace the peace with my Creator the
Almighty God
I will cherish your memories the most valuable gift for me
You will always remain in my heart I love you Adam
My eyes look for you in the sky for the shiny star
The stars that used to be in your eyes
The sparkling stars always reminds
Me the twinkle in your eyes
And cheeky smile
When I close my eyes the star's shine
Your eyes sparkle and your smile shines
I love you Adam I love you Adam
I love you Adam more than you can think
You were my friend my very close friend
You were my son, my eldest son
My heartaches, my eyes cry
My pain is sharp but very special
I wish to feel the sharpness of the pain for the rest of my life
It keeps me close to Allah (SWT) and you
Love you Adam,
More than you know

(Urfana Ayub, 30th November 2010)

A Year Gone By

I don't think words can ever really cover the journey I've endured this past year. I take my mind back to the events of the 27th of December 2009 and it's frightening and even dreamlike how time has flown, yet dragged equally.

My blessed nephew Mohammed Adam Ayub - may he be granted the highest heaven, Ameen, passed away on the 27th of December, 2009. And in my heart the connection to him was a simple, unconditional and heartfelt bond, just as a mother to her child. I feel like he was a son and still 'is' a son to me. You can't put it into words, not always able to describe it justly, but you 'feel it'. And because you feel it, you know it's right and how the Almighty intended it to be, in his wisdom All praise is due to God alone. How fortunate and lucky and blessed was I that I was bestowed such a precious gift so early on in my life, thanks be to God alone.

I have experienced loss before, a friend's mum, a friend's dad, an uncle from Pakistan, my grandparents who I don't quite remember meeting, or a neighbour I met from time to time. All these exposures do give you a very brief insight into death, but it's such a small snapshot, when you have this big spirit, this loving child, this beam of light that draws you close to him. And you watch him grow from this beautiful cuddly baby, to a handsome humble kind hearted man, Thanks be to God Almighty, to then not be with us anymore.

Its world's apart from anything you've experienced in life. I can honestly say that being at the passing of Adam, may his soul be at complete rest, Ameen, was the single worst moment of my life and the best moment in my life. I needed to be there. I know I had to witness it, and if I am honest, if I in some way gave him even a brief moment of comfort in his last hours, then I consider myself to be exceptionally fortunate by God's kind will. Not everyone has that opportunity. I remember that night like it was yesterday. Some things you can never quite convey in words, and if I am honest, that night will be with me forever, along with my last words, moments of comfort and my last embrace of my son.

This year has been full of so many challenges, broken and shattered hearts, tears of sadness, constant moments of comfort shared, smiles given at moments of Adam's reflection. Now knowing that he's gone, there is confusion at times with this world and how we do actually fit in? And a very consistent growth and recognition that we too on this earth are not meant for this earth, but beyond to our maker, our saviour the Almighty God.

I know that a part of my heart died that day and I can't undo that; it's a reality. You are the walking dead because your shell, your body gives the illusion you are alive and living, but inside it's a completely different story, just darkness and emptiness with a true desperation to cling onto any light, no matter how little. But that's when you know things have to change, as that's the only way to survive. One way is remembering all my moments with Adam and that they are equally a reality that I shared and we shared as a family.

People constantly say this person is a true gent; this person is amazing; you can see that they have something about them. I can truly,with my heart and sincerely state that Mohammed Adam Ayub was not of this world. He had a contagious personality that you felt and even needed and wanted to be around. He could warm your heart by just looking at you, give you peace and comfort by hugging you, and you feel that you mattered to him, just by him talking to you. There are not many young people you can say that about. I try to take stock now of 18 years and 7 months of Adam's life and how it integrated into all our lives. But whatever I say, it will always come short, never really truly reflect or do real justice.

This past year has crystallised the gaping hole, the void that one soul can make to a family of so many people, thanks be to God, and many others living in the community, studying alongside him, walking past him in the street. How that presence, once so effortlessly with us, now seems to have disappeared from our eyes, but lives, All praise is due to God alone, in our hearts of hearts.

Adam was missed from every single day of his passing up until the moment the ink goes on this page, and I've no doubt that will continue on and on.

For me, from what I've seen and felt, I've never experienced pain in this way and I've seen my family in a new light. I feel in many ways that we each represent seeds planted in the soil and from time to time we are watered, All praise is due to God alone. So when the passing happened, it was as though the sun shone, with some dark clouds. But nevertheless there was sun and this enabled growth, roots to really blossom, renewed strength, and development, and we have all developed separately and as a family unit in much the same way as a tree. I also feel grateful, All praise is due to God alone, there is a higher level of connection that has happened, and strengthened my relationship with my Maker, All praise is due to God alone.

I remember Him frequently and I fear when I'm not doing the right thing. I realise His instructions are for my benefit. When I look around and see my life, my world, and the people who are close to me, I know that without a shadow of a doubt that I am blessed. And the journey continues on for us all to 'BE' better people, better neighbours, better daughters, better fathers, better humans and ultimately, God willing, better Muslims.

In my heart deep down I know Mohammed Ayub is looked after; he's in a better place than you and I reading this, and I crave for that moment, that if I am fortunate enough, God willing, I will see him again in heaven. And I pray that I can make enough positive change in my life to do that.

I look into his parents' eyes, into my parents' eyes, and I know, although I can't fully grasp their grief, as everyone's grief and loss is so personal - I realise it's a lifetime battle we will have to endure, with or without any armour. The battle is very real and it exists.

Ultimately, may everyone be blessed in life, God willing. I pray that everyone is so fortunate, like my family, to have someone so life enhancing, blessed, loving, non-judgemental, good hearted and God-fearing as part of their own family. We were entrusted with such a precious gift, and we have to, without doubt, realise some gifts are now with us for life – just a fixed term.

Thinking about this year, how one year on, life has changed for me, my family, my nephew's family, my community, I know that the positive effects will, God willing, continue to cause a ripple effect. Death and loss is hard, your heart bleeds, you feel pain you have never felt before, you question life in a way you never did before and you get a shock to the system, that you feel you may never recover from – as all you see is dark clouds ahead. You need to anchor and focus your energies, transfer them to your loved ones, to your spiritual path, to the people and surroundings that matter most to you. And ultimately, if you let go – if you have enough faith to let go and be at the true mercy of your Maker – God willing, you will survive. You may not be that person before the death. You may feel you can't get back to that place again, but survival can also take you to other places, places of comfort and peace and often a bridge to get closer to why and what we are doing on this earth. That bridge, if you want it to be, can take you to God. I am still building my bridge, and with each brick laid, I feel I am getting closer and realising my true path. Adam was more to me than I ever knew, and for many others I see the same. He is irreplaceable and I am not the same person I was before. I know he has, God willing, remoulded me, and I pray, into a stronger, better, kinder, wiser soul who has a renewed wish for all my loved ones to bear this loss with the strength to better our lives for our own hereafter, God willing.

May God help all those people who have encountered loss. May your pain be managed. May you continue to find patience and peace in your prayers, and God willing, May you learn to live a positive and a religious filled life, to the end of your days, Ameen. God rest all those souls no longer with us. May they be granted the highest heaven, Ameen. May their souls be at peace, in the Shade and calmness of the Almighty. May their sins be forgiven and may any reward/good deed be done on their behalf or in response to their character, God willing. May they receive this reward in their favour on the day of Judgement, Ameen.

Simply, I love you Adam and miss you, and although I write this with tears from my eyes and heart, I am soooo thankful for your birth, existence and departure – a true angel amongst us; All praise is due to God alone. Be smiling wherever you are my son.

All my love and prayers until the end of my days...

Xx Your loving Phupie (Farhat)

Adam

When I think about you,
I think about someone so pure and true.
Never did I think you would be the first one to depart,
But I can tell you one thing; you'll always remain in our hearts.
I still can't believe that you've left,
The pain I feel I just can't confess,
You were the heart and soul of the family,
You bought happiness, love and the energy.
If I ever said or did anything to upset you, I'm sorry
I'm sat here remembering the good times,
Automatically they've been memorised,
I'll never forget the things you said,
Your images and thoughts keep playing in my head.
I never in this world thought you'd leave,
I remember you and me.
In our family you were the first boy,
Your entrance bought lightness and joy,
We shared some special things together,
I really thought we would have conversations like them forever.
It was nice to know that you could share the things that you did,
And I could help with some of your decisions,
I'll always remember mine and your revisions.
You'll always be number one, our so called revision used to be fun
Moments like these will be cherished and I'll always remember,
But never did I think you would have to leave this December.
You were rock solid emotionally and physically,
You were always full of energy,
I used to forget sometimes that you used to be poorly.

Everyone misses you because they cared,
They remember what they had and the love that they shared.
They all love you so much,
I can't get over the fact that we'll never get to hear or see or feel your tender sweet touch.
We'll never forget the moments we shared with you,
Everyone that was involved with you,
Was so super true, we'll always love you.
You'd always put a smile on our face as soon as you'd speak,
Never in the world did I think you'd become weak.
You tried so hard not to show that side,
But in your last year and moments you died and everyone cried.
My heart, my body, my soul was dying in pain shouting and screaming,
Because a heart of Gold stop beating.
God had put you out your misery,
He needed your company.
Two twinkling eyes were put to rest,
God ripped our hearts out to prove that he's taken the best.
Can't believe you've gone so far away,
He took you on such a blessed day.
Now when I look up in the sky,
I know you're in heaven up high.
But I'm selfish for crying that you've gone and still wanting you back
I do, but I know that's not going to happen.
Because death was already on your case,
I know you're in a better place.
I've tried so hard to be strong,
But for how long?
Adam everyone's broken down,
I'm the oldest; I have to get rid of those frowns.
I know you'd want that even though you're a million miles
You'd want them all to love, live and always smile.

I had to keep myself in a limit,
When I think of you, I think of your spirit.
For me you're not gone, your spirit is still here,
So I have nothing to fear,
You're closer to us now, than you have ever been,
The only difference is you just can't be seen.
Since you've been gone I feel like death is a bridge to another place,
And heaven is my dream which I have to chase.
I love you and I can't wait to see you,
Don't worry I'm going to look after everyone,
We've lost a soldier/son.
Now I'm the oldest daughter, granddaughter, grandchild and niece
So don't you worry about anything, just rest in peace.

Your loving sister Hina (Adam's Cousin Sister)

A Year On

For the past year the memories of Adam passing away are with me every second, every minute of every day. The loss of Adam has highlighted to me how God has control of life, and he has the power to take people away from this realm when he desires. The strength and courage of Adam over the 18 years has shown to me that he was special and incredibly strong to live with his illness and try to live a normal life.

The heart of Adam was so warm and kind as he made an instant impact to those who knew him. His smile was something that he carried at all times, even when he was suffering inside. He was my younger brother in a lot of ways and when Babur went away, he made sure that Mum and Dad stayed strong, because Adam was similar and so loved, just like Babur.

I look at myself every day and realise that time is so short and my time on this planet could end at any second. I am sure that Adam is sat in paradise, God willing, looking down on all of us, saying I will be here when we all leave. God willing, my deen is strong, but I need to concentrate every second and minute and not lose focus as I want to be with Adam and all the other good and special people that are in Paradise, God willing.

The loss of any person is never good, but I pray that Adam has made people aware that our life on this planet is in the hands of God, and we all need to look at ourselves to see how his death will or has changed us. I pray for everybody in my prayers that we all follow the right path and make sure that we stay away from sinful acts. Adam has shown to all of us that if your mind is clear and your heart is pure, then God will answer your prayers. God will do what is best for you, and sometimes it can be hard to see what he has done, but it might be for a good reason.

My brother Adam, please look upon us all and make sure that we stay away from evil doings and follow the deen path. Adam, you showed how strong and kind a young person can be, and God willing, we all should learn from you. The day will come when I will follow you, and pray for me that I am forgiven for all my bad sins and that I am with you in paradise. Adam, you brought 18 years of wonderful memories to all of us and the memories will stay with us to the day we leave. We will have tough times, but not like the ones you lived with, so we should be grateful and look at things around us to see how lucky we are. God willing, I will see you when I am required, but keep an eye on all of us in the meantime.

Yours lovingly ChaCha Yousaf (Adam's paternal uncle)

Taking It All for Granted

We take for granted
Each passing day
Each person, each thing
Which does come our way

We take for
granted
Life, air, love
The plants, the earth
The heaven above

We take for granted
Our families
Our homes, our souls
Our faculties

We take for granted
Everything
Only realise
Only think
When God takes back
One of these things
How much we need it all

And then-cry and plead as we may
There is no second chance
No simple retake
No backward glance
For once the things
We love are gone
And we are left
So utterly alone
Only then we do realise

How much we cared
How much we miss all of this

Only then do we see
How much better we'd feel
How much better we'd spare
To thank, to love, to praise the One
Who gave it all to us

(Nasreen A Juneja. London)

You Can Shed Tears That He Is Gone

You can shed tears that he is gone or
You can smile that he has lived
You can close your eyes and pray that he will come back
Or you can open your eyes and see all that he has left
Your heart can be empty because you can't see him
Or you can be truthful of the love you shared
You can turn your back on tomorrow and live yesterday
Or you can be happy for tomorrow because of yesterday
You can remember him and only that he is gone
Or you can cherish his memory and let it live on
You can cry and close your mind
Be empty and turn your back
Or you can do what he'd want
Open your eyes love and go on

(unknown poet)

In the short time you were part of my life, you have brought us closer as a family and closer to God. I have also grown stronger knowing how brave you were and how humble you were. I will always love you and the only way I can show you this is by praying to Allah (SWT) for you. May God grant you the highest heaven, Ameen.

(Babur - Adam's paternal uncle)

Life after Mohammed Adam Ayub went back to God; life's not the same. I miss him so much. Nothing can prepare you for death or losing a loved one. I think of death every day. Knowing that you could be the next to go is very scary. Are we prepared? The truth is no. We are too wrapped in this world. We need to cherish life every day. Be grateful and thankful for what you have. Not to be greedy for materialistic things. One big thing I have noticed since Adam left us is all our family coming closer together. I hope this bond stays for many years to come. I pray Allah (SWT) gives strength and patience to Adam's parents, grandparents, brothers, sister, aunts and uncles, cousins, brothers and sisters to learn and turn to Islam and God for guidance, Ameen.

(Abid – Adam's paternal uncle)

"You can die anytime."

(Ahmad – Adam's youngest brother)

"After Adam's death I have learnt anyone can go at any time and we can't change anything, we are powerless."

(Arslan – Adam's brother)

"After Adam was gone, I realised anybody can die at any time, so live your life as it's your last day."

(Ambar – Adam's only sister)

"The whole family have a reason for living and thanking God

195

for His blessings. Families and people have become closer after contact was lost. He reunited us."

(Mohammed Ayub – Adam's father)

"It reminds me of my death."

(Ayesha – cousin sister)

"His death has brought family closer and I have learned that it only takes a second to die."

(Bilal – cousin brother)

"We should not get too busy in this world. Allah (SWT) can take us anytime."

(Zeenat - Aunty)

"I have been reading more prayer and reciting Quran."

(Kanwal- cousin sister)

A Smile Lives On

Adam's smile was no doubt God's blessing. He left his smile etched in everyone's memories. To smile at someone is a good deed. Maybe people will remember you by your smile after you have passed away. If it is not a habit of yours to smile, then make it so. Zain Bhikha's poem translates my innermost feelings:

I Remember Your Smile

Where there is a right, there is no wrong,
I always thought we were so strong,
But our time just flew by,
There wasn't a chance to say goodbye.

Am so confused,
I feel all alone,
Deep in my heart,
I know Allah has called you home.
But yea your smile still lingers in my mind,
And yea it's so hard I just break down and cry.

I remember the time our friendship was strong,
I remember your eyes find a way to melt my heart,
Most of all I remember your smile.

Sometimes I lie awake at night,
The pain in my heart, I just can't fight
Why did you have to go away?
Yet I know none of us can stay you will always be so special to
me.

In the world you will always live as a memory,

But yea your smile still lingers in my mind,
And yea its so hard I just break down,
And cry I remember our friendship was strong,
I remember your eyes find a way to melt my heart.
Most of all I remember your smile.

(Zain Bhikha Album -1415 the Beginning - 2009)

A Message From My Adam

To Those Whom I Love And Those Who Love Me

When I am gone, release me, let me go
I have so many things to see and do
You must not tie yourself to me with tears
Be happy that I have had so many years

I gave you my love, you can only guess
How much you gave me in happiness
I thank you for the love each have shown
But now it is time I travelled on alone

So grieve a while for me, if grieve you must
Then let your grief be comforted by trust
It is only for a while that we must part
So bless the memories in your heart

I will not be far away, for life goes on
So if you need me, call and I will come

Though you cannot see or touch me, I will be near
And if you listen with your heart, you will hear
All of my love around you soft and clear

Then, when you must come this way alone
I will greet you with a smile and a Welcome Home
(Unknown poet)

Translator's Note

It has been an honour and pleasure to participate in the translation of Taray Janay Kay Baad "After You Were Gone".

The author, Mrs. Urfana Ayub, is a very courageous lady who not only bore the death of her young son with resilience and patience and has got on with her own life, but today, working in the community, she is helping other women who have gone through tragedy or trauma in their lives.

When she began writing she did not intend to write a book. In fact she started writing it as a diary and it was only when she realised her writing can help others who are going through or been through similar loss.

Mrs. Ayub is not a professional writer, but her words in this book and her follow on book Maray Khat Taray Naam "My Letters to You" reflect her literary talent.

The original version was written in Urdu. Though I have tried my best to express Mrs. Ayub's emotions in English; for those of you who understand Urdu I would strongly encourage you to read the original version too.

The entire income of this book will be going to charity work which will be a Sadaqa e Jariya (source of eternal reward) for the late *Mohammed Adam Ayub*. By purchasing your copy of this book, you are also sharing in this charity reward."

Dr Zahid Hussain - Translator

Editor's Note

This story of a mother's grief at the death of her young son is movingly told and written from the heart. Some of the language describing her relationship with her child and her feelings is truly beautiful.

The book follows the course of Urfana Ayub's first year after Adam's death, showing how her faith helped her to cope and also opened up a new chapter in her life and a new vocation as a writer. Because the book is in the form of diary entries, readers will take this highly personal journey alongside Adam's bereaved mother.

I learned a lot from editing the book and, as a mother of children around the same age as Adam, could relate to many of Urfana's sentiments. It was courageous of Adam's mum to share all her fears, challenges, sleepless nights and poetry in order to help other parents.

Siobhan Dignan - Editor

About the Author

Mrs. Urfana Ayub is Pakistani by birth, now settled in Bradford, UK since 1990.

As a qualified Social Worker, Interpreter, Translator and Counsellor, she is actively engaged with people, their problems and emotions. This work has enabled her to see life very closely and given her a wider experience of the problems faced by families and their reactions. At the same time her profession has also given her the insight to see beyond the "outer face", into the souls of others. All these experiences have added depth to Urfana's writing. Her command of language and expression are proof of the effects of her profession, as she has never written before in her life.

Urfana Ayub possesses a very positive personality and has the rare talent of seeing good in every person and situation. This quality has helped her immensely to bear the tragedy of losing her son and redirect her life on a new path.

Acknowledgements

I wish to thank my creator for giving me the opportunity to express myself through writing this book. My heartfelt thanks to my family for their love and support. To my dear friend and husband Ayub, my children Arslan, Ambar and Ahmad. My sincere respect to my parents and rest of my family.

I also extend my gratitude to Dr Samira Haque, Dr Zahid Hussain, Zahida Ishaque, Rabia Umar, Kashif Ishaq, Samreen Ghafoor, Farooq Bhai, Maria, my editor Siobhan Dignan, and all those people who have encouraged me to get this book translated into English.

But above all, I will always be grateful to someone very special humble personality, a very genuine, unique and kind hearted individual who wishes to remain nameless, for ensuring that the task of translating the book never became a lonely ordeal for me.

My utmost appreciation to all those who have worked and contributed in this project.

In memory of my son, my **MOHAMMED ADAM AYUB**

Urfana Ayub

Supplication for the deceased at the funeral prayer

اللّٰهُمَّ اغْفِرْ لَهُ وَارْحَمْهُ، وَعَافِهِ،
وَاعْفُ عَنْهُ وَأَكْرِمْ نُزُلَهُ وَوَسِّعْ
مُدْخَلَهُ، وَاغْسِلْهُ بِالْمَاءِ وَالثَّلْجِ
وَالْبَرَدِ، وَنَقِّهِ مِنَ الْخَطَايَا كَمَا نَقَّيْتَ
الثَّوْبَ الْأَبْيَضَ مِنَ الدَّنَسِ، وَأَبْدِلْهُ
دَارًا خَيْرًا مِنْ دَارِهِ وَأَهْلًا خَيْرًا مِنْ
أَهْلِهِ وَزَوْجًا خَيْرًا مِنْ زَوْجِهِ،
وَأَدْخِلْهُ الْجَنَّةَ، وَأَعِذْهُ مِنْ عَذَابِ
الْقَبْرِ وَعَذَابِ النَّارِ.

'O Allah, forgive and have mercy upon him, excuse him and pardon him, and make honourable his reception. Expand his entry, and cleanse him with water, snow, and ice, and purify him of sin as a white robe is purified of filth. Exchange his home for a better home, and his family for a better family, and his spouse for a better spouse. Admit him into the garden, protect him from the punishment of the grave and the torment of the Fire' (Ameen).

Glossary

SWT -Subhan wa Ta'alla meaning the Glorified and Almighty

Makkah -The birth place of Prophet Muhammad (PBUH), the city where the Kaa'ba is where Muslims go for Hajj

Masjid -e- Nabawi -The Holy Mosque, initially built by Prophet Muhammad in Madina (PBUH)

Eid ul Fitr -Religious festival of The Muslim, celebrated at the end of Holy month of Ramadhan

Eid ul Ad'ha -Religious festival of The Muslim, celebrated on 10th of Zilhaj the last month of Islamic calendar

Ammi -Title used for one's mother, but in this book it refers in most places to my mother in law, who is like a mother to me.

Mamoon -Maternal Uncle

Abbu -A tile used for one's father, but I call Ayub's father also with that name.

Baba -Literally meaning old man, but affectionate title used sometimes for father and sometimes for grandfather

Phuphie -Father's sister

Aab e Zam Zam -The holy water obtained from the holy well of Zam Zam in Makkah

Kalima Shahadah -Kalima (Shahadah) - One of the five pillars of Islam meaning "There is no God but Allah, Mohammad (Peace be Upon Him) is his messenger.

Bhai - Brother

Masjid -Mosque

Asr -The prayer offered between mid afternoon and sunset

Maghrib -The prayer offered just after sunset.

Isha -The prayer offered about one and a half hour of sunset when the darkness has set in.

Dada Abbu -Paternal Grandfather

Dadi Ammi -Paternal Grandmother

Nani - Maternal Grandmother

Chachcha -Father's brother/paternal uncle

InshaAllah -By the will of Allah (SWT)

Khala - Mother's sister

Nasheed -Islamic religious song

Tasbeeh -Rosary beeds

Roza -Mausoleum